Women in American Education, 1820–1955

Recent Titles in
Contributions to the Study of Education

Women in American Education, 1820–1955

The Female Force and Educational Reform

JUNE EDWARDS

Contributions to the Study of Education, Number 81

GREENWOOD PRESS
Westport, Connecticut • London

Library of Congress Cataloging-in-Publication Data

Edwards, June, 1934–
    Women in American education, 1820–1955 : the female force and educational reform /
June Edwards.
      p. cm.—(Contributions to the study of education, ISSN 0196–707X ; no. 81)
    Includes bibliographical references and index.
    ISBN 0–313–31947–2 (alk. paper)
    1. Women in education—United States—History. 2. Women educators—United
States—Biography. 3. Educational change—United States—History.
    I. Title. II. Series.
    LC1757.E39 2002
    370′.82—dc21   2001045122

British Library Cataloguing in Publication Data is available.

Library of Congress Catalog Card Number: 2001045122
ISBN: 0–313–31947–2
ISSN: 0196–707X

First published in 2002

Greenwood Press, 88 Post Road West, Westport, CT 06881
An imprint of Greenwood Publishing Group, Inc.
www.greenwood.com

Printed in the United States of America

The paper used in this book complies with the
Permanent Paper Standard issued by the National
Information Standards Organization (Z39.48–1984).

10 9 8 7 6 5 4 3 2 1

In memory of my mother,
Katharine Rose Kirkhuff,
a schoolteacher in Geary, Oklahoma,
1909–1912

Contents

Introduction

A contemporary term called *Constructivism* is widely accepted in educational theory as the best means of engendering true education. To understand subject matter and make meaningful connections, students build on prior knowledge, do open-ended research, solve problems, take risks, experiment, create, draw conclusions, and apply what they have learned to new situations. Active engagement is the key. In this method of learning, students assume much more responsibility than in traditional classrooms and often work in small groups. They participate in community life and contribute useful service. The teacher's role, although still crucial, shifts from center stage to that of guide, facilitator, motivator, and friend.

Constructivist reforms are indeed an excellent infusion into modern-day schools, but the methods involved are not at all new. The focus of this book is on eight women who successfully utilized many of these practices in earlier times and made significant contributions not only to American education but to society as a whole. They were not the first or only ones, of course. Predecessors and contemporaries such as Jan Comenius, Jean Jacques Rousseau, Johann Pestalozzi, Friedrich Froebel, John Dewey, Booker T.

Washington, and W.E.B. DuBois also left their marks. However, these male philosophers and educators have been duly and deservingly celebrated. The females noted here, although they were well-known and respected in their own day, are often missing from current books on education, given short shrift, or not depicted as groundbreakers, for a variety of reasons.

First, of course, is the age-old prejudice against females in all areas. Although this has improved in recent years, especially with the addition of women's studies in college curriculums, many philosophy, history, and foundations of education texts have not changed significantly except to add a few women to the discussion or mention their names in passing. The ones selected for this book have been written about extensively in other contexts, but are still unknown to many students in education programs. Those who want to be kindergarten teachers, for instance, often have never heard of Elizabeth Peabody. Those interested in human ecology (formerly called home economics) do not learn of Ellen Swallow Richards until their advanced courses in that area.

Second, although the beliefs and practices of these women challenged the theories of the White male educators of their day, their teaching strategies are rarely described as a radical break with tradition. For example, Catharine Beecher has been extolled for the establishment of academic schools for girls and training programs for teachers, but the innovative methods used in her institutions have been ignored. Also, her well received home management guidebooks are seldom viewed as having educational significance. Such women's unique and sometimes revolutionary contributions, if mentioned at all, are diminished as peripheral to those of more famous men.

Third, these women educators have not been considered as important, perhaps, because of whom they chose to serve. They elected to work with those the establishment had rejected or deemed not worthy of education: the very young, the mentally disabled, the immigrant poor, teenaged girls (White and Black), young women seeking higher education and careers, housewives who needed homemaking skills, and female scientists, teachers, nurses, and doctors. Not only did these women believe in the potential of their clients, but they used teaching methods that were innovative and highly effective, some of which, wrapped in new skins, are being touted as "modern-day reforms." Their methods focused on student interests and involvement, incorporated multiple skills, stressed open-ended research, critical thinking, and integration of subject matters, and promoted peer cooperation and shared teacher–student decision making. Today, we would call these strategies student-centered instruction, holistic teaching, cooperative learning, and teacher facilitation. In short, Constructivism. Their practices were radical in their day—and still are.

The eight women in this book were selected because they chose to or were forced to work outside the traditional White male-dominated institutions, because their philosophies were antithetical to what was usually being done, or because they wanted to expand education to clientele not reached by traditional schooling. They also wrote articles and books that promoted their beliefs and methods, which are helpful today in understanding the historical period and the social restrictions that often hampered their work. Excerpts from these publications illustrate the women's goals, concerns, and challenges.

Each chapter in this book contains a biographical sketch of an educator's life and describes the reasons she embarked on her trailblazing endeavors, the hardships and hurdles encountered, her educational theories and methods, some criticisms voiced by contemporaries and present-day scholars, and her long lasting achievements. The women are as follow:

1. **Catharine Esther Beecher** (1800–1878). Perhaps the best-known woman in her day, Beecher established two secondary schools for girls and wrote much appreciated domestic education books for adult women homemakers. She also recruited and trained female teachers for public schools in the West, thus changing school teaching from a male occupation to a respectable career for educated women, and enforced the belief that good teaching requires pedagogical as well as academic knowledge.

2. **Elizabeth Palmer Peabody** (1804–1887). A leader in the intellectual Transcendentalist group that included such luminaries as Margaret Fuller and Ralph Waldo Emerson, Peabody in young adulthood taught in and wrote about Bronson Alcott's nontraditional school in Boston, then branched out on her own. In her later years, she became entranced with Friedrich Froebel's work in Germany and established the first English-speaking kindergarten in America. For the next 30 years she trained teachers for these schools and promoted, through writings and speeches, the essential features of early childhood education.

3. **Elizabeth Blackwell** (1820–1910). The first woman to graduate from a regular medical school in America, Blackwell gave daring but well-received lectures on health and hygiene for girls and women.

Because most medical schools and hospitals still barred female students and doctors, she established a woman's hospital and medical training school in New York City, promoted sanitation in hospitals and homes—a revolutionary idea in its day—and helped establish a medical school for women in London.

4. **Ellen Swallow Richards** (1842–1911). The first woman chemist in America and first female graduate and faculty member at the Massachusetts Institute of Technology (MIT), Richards conducted laboratory training for female science teachers, helped to establish the Woods Hole, Massachusetts, Marine Biological Laboratory, and encouraged other females to undertake science careers. She became nationally famous for her outstanding work on environmental issues and is credited with starting the ecology movement in the United States (even coining the word *oekology*). Today, she is most known for establishing the national Home Economics Association and promoting such courses in secondary schools and colleges as a means of improving home and family life through applied science.

5. **Jane Addams** (1860–1935). A well-to-do social reformer, Addams established a settlement house called Hull-House to give aid and education to immigrant adults and children living in the slums of Southside Chicago. Active on the school board and other political entities, she fought for child labor laws, compulsory education, and improved sanitation in housing, streets, and schools. Hull-House became an educational, cultural, and social center that celebrated the contributions and arts of the diverse immigrants while helping them learn English and improve their lives in America.

6. **Maria Montessori** (1870–1952). Although Montessori was an Italian and her schools originated in Italy, they were soon brought to the United States where they still flourish, but have been somewhat redesigned to fit American culture and goals for young children. A psychiatrist and the first woman in Italy to graduate from medical school, Montessori initially became famous for her work with mentally disabled children who had been confined in insane asylums. After designing self-correcting materials and creating the "Montessori Method" that taught children to be independent, responsible, and cooperative, she established a teacher-training institution in Italy that supplied teachers for her worldwide schools. She came several times to America in the early 1900s to promote them.

7. **Mary McLeod Bethune** (1875–1955). The daughter of freed slaves, Bethune established a boarding school for African-American girls in Florida and taught her students both academic subjects and vocational skills so they would be economically self-sufficient. The school was later joined with a male institution and became Bethune–

Cookman College, with Bethune as president. She established the national Colored Woman's Association, which helped ex-slaves gain education, jobs, and decent housing. In 1938, Bethune was appointed by President Franklin D. Roosevelt to be director of Negro Affairs in the National Youth Administration, the first African-American woman to serve in a government post. She was close friends with Eleanor Roosevelt and the recipient of many awards for her national leadership in education and civil rights.

8. **Helen Parkhurst** (1887–1973). An American disciple of Maria Montessori, Parkhurst eventually parted ways and designed her own individualized approach for secondary students called the Dalton Laboratory Plan. This unique method required a total restructuring of schools into experimental laboratories that eliminated lockstep grades and rigid, time-bound classes. It emphasized individual interests and promoted student decision making, responsibility, creativity, and cooperation. The Laboratory Plan, which contrasted sharply with traditional U.S. schools of the 1920s and 1930s, became even more popular in other countries, such as China, Japan, and Denmark. The Dalton School that she established in New York City in 1919 still enjoys an outstanding reputation as an academic institution where individuality and creativity flourish.

Although each of these women contributed something different to U.S. education, they had common bonds in their experiences, personalities, and aims. First was their great determination to obtain an education for themselves and pursue nontraditional goals, despite official and social barriers that kept most women at home and out of public light. They also possessed amazing self-confidence and courage, which pushed them forward in the face of hostility, disappointments, and sometimes poor health. Where did this indomitable will come from? In each case, the women's families were well-respected in their communities. The Peabodys, Beechers, and Blackwells—parents and siblings—were remarkably talented and outspoken. Jane Addams's father was a state senator and wealthy mill owner, and the parents of Richards, Bethune, Montessori, and Parkhurst were local leaders and supportive of education for their daughters.

Birth order may also have been a contributing factor. Some of the women were either an only child or an older sibling who took on adult responsibilities at a young age, partly due to the death or illness of a parent. Because of their wit and spunk, many were their father's favorite, but they also received strong support from their mothers, who often were self-educated, very capable, and in some cases the more stable parent. If there were boys in the family, the girls were seen as having equal value, although equal opportunities were not available.

However, animosity against women speaking in public and taking leadership roles was rampant and degrading, especially for those living in the nineteenth century, and sometimes physically threatening. To avoid this problem, Catharine Beecher had her public lectures read by a male relative or friend. Others refused to cave in to societal pressure and were castigated for speaking to mixed audiences and on subjects that challenged prevailing beliefs or values. They were often denied a platform, except with exclusively women's groups.

The women were also resolute in their goals to improve the lives of people of all ages—educationally, physically, economically, socially, and spiritually—and in seeking justice, civil rights, and career opportunities for those who lacked the power, knowledge, and skills to help themselves. For these leaders, learning went far beyond school walls and encompassed all of life from birth to death. They saw education as an expansion of other aspects of life and not as a separate entity, and became involved in politics and social issues in order to improve the well-being of all people, but especially women, children, the underclass, and the downtrodden.

Additionally, the women strove vigorously, but not always successfully, to be accepted as full-fledged professionals in their fields. The bias against female doctors, teachers, scientists, college professors, and administrators was demeaning and sometimes vicious. Never too proud or aloof to do the everyday labor required, these women taught classes, trained teachers, gave lectures, traveled the country to raise funds for their schools and projects, fought for legislation to protect their clients' rights and welfare, and often became a thorn in the flesh to those in power.

This willingness to speak out and do the hard, tedious work, although it helped to disseminate their ideas and brought them public admiration, probably undercut their stature as intellectuals. It also led to their later dismissal by many education historians and textbook writers as minor figures who contributed little unique or substantial to educational philosophy. Practitioners are seldom as prized as pure thinkers.

The strongest support for the female educators' work came from well-to-do women, who, wanting more opportunities for their daughters, gave time and money to raise funds, publicize lectures, and promote the activities of these leaders. But they also received valuable assistance and encouragement from some of the men in their lives: a father, brother, husband, or friend; a few highly respected men who risked their own reputations to aid the women's activities; and several wealthy men who made generous contributions to their schools and projects.

All of the women described here pursued their self-chosen career at considerable cost to their personal lives and well-being. Unlike men, they had to make choices, sometimes very painful ones. Perhaps the most difficult was the decision to have a demanding career rather than husband, children, and home. Although they deliberately selected nontraditional paths for themselves and encouraged other women to do so, they each believed that child care and home management was highly valuable work, not only for women but for men. Well-run homes and well-nurtured children benefited society as well as the individual families.

Most of them, however, had no homes of their own in the traditional sense. Some moved around from one relative or friend to another, sometimes wearing out their welcome. Most did not marry, although several had early loves who either died young or whom they rejected. One had an illegitimate child, but knowing it would destroy her career, kept it a secret and placed the boy with a farm family to raise until he was grown and her reputation as an outstanding educator was secure. One married and had a child, but lived apart from her husband most of her life; another married but remained childless, although she had a lovely home in which she utilized the most advanced management principles and technology; and another adopted an orphan girl who remained her devoted life-long assistant and companion.

These educators felt that marriage, children, and a good home life were important, but in their day could not be combined with a career, at least not to the extent that they wanted. There were good reasons for their choices. In many ways, women were better off single. Married women in earlier times had no legal rights, even to their children. Middle-class women often had large families, thus spending most of their lives pregnant and supervising children and servants. Early schooling was usually done at home, which also required time and expertise on the part of the mother. Children were frequently ill and many died. Married women themselves were often in poor health and died at a young age from diseases or childbirth.

The women discussed here believed that the "average" female should spend her life as a wife, mother, and homemaker. But none viewed themselves as average, and so felt justified in defying conventional rules. For them, the drive to attain intellectual achievements and serve the larger community was far stronger than the desire for domestic life. They felt firmly that women should have the right to pursue whatever goals fit their talents and should be respected for their contributions, whether in a profession or at home.

However, without a husband to supply financial support, most spent vast amounts of time and energy raising funds to keep themselves and their educational projects alive. This stress drained their minds, bodies, and spirits and interfered with the need to provide leadership to the institutions they established. Debilitating depression and various body ailments also took their toll on the mental and physical well-being of these women. Despite this, they unselfishly helped make the way easier for other females who wanted to have careers beyond homemaking. They opened schools, shared knowledge, fought for civil rights, education, and professional opportunities and gave leadership to national organizations that dealt with women's issues.

Finally, a common element among these women was the role that religious faith played in their educational beliefs and practices. Although raised in various Protestant churches, most took from their particular denomination what spoke to their soul and affirmed them as creative, talented leaders. They ignored the parts that rejected female intelligence and worth or that demanded that women submit to male authority and not assume public roles. This sometimes meant repudiating the Calvinistic dogma of the church of their youth or of religious institutions altogether. Most were not particularly devoted to or hampered by any particular creed, but were open to many ideas, both religious and secular. Their friendships included people of all religious persuasions.

However, each woman still believed that education was by nature religious and they maintained a spiritual base in their teaching methods and relationship with students, young and old. They stressed the worth and uniqueness of each individual child, the need for humane and caring teachers, the importance of ethical values, and the joy of learning and growing. They developed and practiced, mostly by intuition, the kinds of teaching methods that today are heralded as "radical new reforms," promoted the idea that all people can learn, accepted and celebrated the many facets of diversity, created educational opportunities for all ages, and demonstrated in their own lives a commitment to lifelong learning, risk-taking, and service.

My hope is that readers, in learning about these educators' contributions and lives, will appreciate the inimitable courage they exhibited and the personal sacrifices they made in the face of official and societal discrimination and economic hardships. Many of us today, I suspect, would give up our goals rather than suffer the degradation, poverty, and outright hostility they frequently experienced, or the years of fighting bureaucratic and social barriers. Reading the biographies and excerpts of these remarkable women, I believe, will give one insight into the times in which they lived and great inspiration for how to live more fully in our own.

1

Catharine Beecher: Educating Girls, Homemakers, and Teachers

Few education institutions of any kind existed for females in the early 1800s. Of what use, according to prevailing thought, were Latin and geometry to those whose primary work would be the home and family? Some girls were taught at least elementary subjects by relatives at home, a few wealthy ones attended finishing schools to learn social graces, and a pioneer effort was begun by Emma Willard in Troy, New York, to give upper and middle-class White girls an education similar to that offered their brothers. Joining this crusade was a spirited, hard-working, assertive young woman named Catharine Esther Beecher.

Beecher did not spurn the teaching of domestic and creative arts; in fact, she urged their inclusion. However, she worked lifelong to counteract a view of femininity that downgraded female intelligence and abilities and fostered poor health. Following her initial success in establishing schools for girls, she branched out to persuade adult middle-class women to treat their work in taking care of family and home as a serious profession. Beecher's books and articles on domestic guidance were enormously popular, for she taught women how to make homemaking an intelligent, creative endeavor rather than dull drudgery. Her sensible advice on child care, nutrition, exercise, sanitation, and home ventilation greatly influenced the move toward more healthful living.

Beecher's third major contribution was the recruiting and training of female teachers for the emerging western states, which not only helped advance the establishment of public schools, but gave unmarried females a respectable way to use their talents and become economically independent (albeit at very low wages). Although Beecher is often criticized for her refusal to support women's suffrage and for advocating the submission of wives to their husbands, she did much to elevate the domestic duties of middle-class women to a dignified career and give them pride in their work. For those who were single, she opened a respectable, challenging career in teaching that allowed them to be self-supporting rather than dependent on male relatives for survival.

EARLY YEARS

Catharine Esther Beecher was born in 1800 into what became one of the most prominent families of the time. Her father, Lyman Beecher, was a famous Congregational minister; her sister, Harriet Beecher Stowe, wrote the influential antislavery book *Uncle Tom's Cabin*; her brother, Henry Ward Beecher, was at one time the most popular preacher in America; and her youngest sister, Isabella Beecher Hooker, was a militant supporter of the women's suffrage movement. There were thirteen Beecher children from Lyman's three successive wives, and almost all were productive, highly respected citizens. Besides those mentioned here, several were preachers and one was a college president.

Lyman Beecher, the father, was a staunch Calvinist, strict but loving with his children. He encouraged them to read widely and write essays and poetry. As the eldest, Catharine received his special attention. Her mother opened a school for girls in their home to supplement her husband's meager income, but died when Catharine was sixteen years old, leaving her for a time in charge of eight younger children, including a small baby, until help came from a maiden aunt and then a stepmother.

Catharine's education came mostly from family members until she entered Miss Pierce's Institution, a finishing school for young ladies. This experience convinced her of the need for a curriculum for females that challenged their intellectual abilities. In her early twenties, she was engaged to a brilliant young mathematics professor at Yale University who drowned in a shipwreck on his way home from Europe. Devastated by this tragedy, Catharine never married and instead devoted her life to educating girls, instructing adult females about intelligent homemaking, and preparing young women for teaching in the burgeoning common schools established in the frontier states.

THE HARTFORD FEMALE SEMINARY

In 1823, Catharine Beecher began her first school in Hartford, Connecticut, with a handful of girls of varying ages. When she asked for public funding, the leading men of Hartford were scornful of teaching girls the same subjects as male students, but several prominent women supported her efforts. In her memoirs, "Educational Reminiscences," she wrote, "This was my first experience of the moral power and good judgment of American women, which has been my chief reliance ever since" (Sklar, 75). The school began in a church basement where two teachers taught nearly one hundred students in one room with no blackboard, maps, or other teaching tools. Despite this, the school was regarded as one of the best in the land for females and in a few years was able to move into its own building with 150 students and eight teachers.

In order for the school to achieve the same respectability as those for boys, grammar, geography, rhetoric, natural philosophy, chemistry, ancient and modern history, anthropology, algebra, geometry, theology and Latin were offered—all initially taught by the two teachers who barely kept ahead of their pupils. Although she instituted this classical curriculum, Beecher believed that most of the girls would marry and thus courses in "domestic science" would not only be practical but would teach thinking and judgment as well as academic subjects. There was no time, space, or equipment, however, to include them.

Beecher tried but failed to have enough teachers educated in different disciplines so they could specialize like those in male schools and colleges. Her financial supporters, however, saw no reason for such extravagance and considered one teacher enough, for instance, to teach all the branches of the sciences—without books, sufficient background, or materials. The strain of running this school took its toll on Beecher's health. Forced to organize and raise funds as well as teach, she left after four years in a state of nervous exhaustion.

Her father and younger siblings had moved to Cincinnati where she joined them to recuperate. The Hartford school continued for another sixty years, but never received the same prominence as under her guidance.

Not long after her arrival in Cincinnati, Beecher established another girls' school, which she called the Western Female Institute. Money was raised for a building, furniture, and materials. She included a new idea—a co-equal faculty, with no one designated as head or director. Unfortunately, however, her controlling and sometimes inconsiderate behavior offended the staff and wealthy townsmen, who soon withdrew their support.

Ambitious, outspoken women were, of course, abhorred by many people in that Victorian age, but even Catharine's family and friends found her frequently trying. When the school closed after only four years, Beecher was almost forty and deeply depressed. Hard-working and energetic much of the time, she suffered periodically from health and mental problems, which she tried to alleviate at "water cure" health spas, the favored recourse for middle- and upper class women. Despite the school's failure and her depression, the years in Cincinnati were fruitful, for it was here that she began her many works on domestic education. By this time she had published a half dozen books on various subjects and established a reputation as one of America's leading educators.

TEACHING METHODS: CRITICAL THINKING, INTEGRATED LEARNING

Although Catharine Beecher was greatly admired by her pupils, like all teachers she had to struggle with problems of discipline, motivation, a wide diversity of pupil abilities, and too little time to teach subjects thoroughly. What she spurned was rote learning, the prevalent practice in most schools at the time. Instead of testing the girls on what they had memorized, she had them explain, illustrate, and apply their knowledge—in other words, to utilize advanced thinking skills. She also believed that subjects such as geography, history, composition, and literature should be integrated, rather than taught as isolated disciplines.

The aim of the curriculum was to teach investigation and reasoning, moral principles, and useful knowledge. The girls were allowed to progress as fast in each subject as they could and to participate in self-government, a student bank, science experiments, plays, and dances. Original compositions were encouraged and visual materials frequently used. With mathematics assignments, students were required to not only solve problems but to explain their thinking process to their classmates. Religious life and deportment were tightly controlled, as was expected at that time, but freedom of inquiry, thought, and creativity flourished in Beecher's schools.

Despite the large student–teacher ratio, stress was placed on guidance and counseling. Where possible, small discussions were held. Teachers met regularly after school with individual students. Physical activity was also emphasized—in a day when females were supposed to be delicate, modest, and weak. To avoid parental disapproval, particularly from upper class mothers, physical exercises were labeled "drills" and accompanied by music to develop grace and posture.

In a later book, *The American Woman's Home* (1869), Beecher objected to "fragile, easily-fatigued, languid girls of a modern age, drilled in book-learning, ignorant of common things" (317–318). At great risk, because her pupils came mostly from affluent families, she successfully instituted learning methods and a curriculum that deviated from the prevailing feminine ideal and made education for girls challenging, engaging, and worthwhile.

DOMESTIC EDUCATION FOR BETTER LIVING

In the 1800s, the health of women was particularly poor, both in cities and on farms. To the upper and middle class, ideal females were pale, fragile flowers who read little, exercised less, and gave no thought to worldly matters. They also married early, had numerous children, aged quickly, and died young. Many men, like Catharine Beecher's father, outlived three or more wives. Beecher was convinced that education about nutrition, exercise, home, and child care was badly needed.

In America at that time, meals were cooked in heavy grease and limited in variety. Wood-burning stoves in poorly ventilated houses poisoned the air with carbon monoxide. Epidemics of cholera and yellow fever killed whole families, and childhood deaths from many causes were common. Medical treatment consisted of bleeding and laxatives, which did more harm than good. Sanitation, even in hospitals, was poor or nonexistent. Clothing, especially for women and children, was heavy and tight-fitting, restricting breath and movement.

Beecher urged mothers to dress children in fewer underclothes so they could more easily run and jump. In her book, *Letters to the People on Health and Happiness* (1856), she stressed physical activity and wrote that parents were bringing up a generation to be "feeble, deformed, homely, sickly, and miserable" (Goodsell, 216). Most children, she said, were too pale and delicate, instead of strong and healthy. Mothers should encourage more exercise and learn about nutrition and good habits.

Like other outstanding female educators, Catharine Beecher believed that teaching was not confined to the classroom but took place in many spheres of life. Her books, such as *Miss Beecher's Domestic Receipt Book* (1846), *The American Woman's Home* (1869), and *Miss Beecher's Housekeeper and Healthkeeper* (1873), educated millions of women about home management, child care, and moral living. Although aimed at females, her target was also children and men. "Let the women of a country be made virtuous and intelligent," Beecher wrote, "and the men will certainly be the same" (1841, 9).

The moral leadership and salvation of a society, she believed, came primarily from the home, and the central figure in that home—the woman—needed knowledge and good judgment that came from education, not just experience. Providing this education was a major goal of her life. "Every woman," she wrote, "should imbibe, from early youth, the impression that she is in training for the discharge of the most important, the most difficult, and the most sacred and interesting duties that can possibly employ the highest intellect" (1869, 221).

Catharine Beecher's books on domestic science contained a large body of knowledge, presented in a readable and interesting style. Given that her only hands-on experience came from a few years as a teenager helping to raise siblings, the information and advice she gave women was amazingly enlightened. Her books covered almost every domestic activity, including the raising of happy and healthy children, proper ventilation, food preparation, gardening, and interior decorating—almost none of which she had personally practiced. However, her research was thorough, her suggestions sensible, and the respect for readers so evident that they seemed not to know or care that she was an unmarried, childless, sometimes cantankerous woman, often debilitated by ill-health, who moved frequently from one relative's house to another. To the public, "Miss Beecher" was one of the best-known and most admired women in America.

EDUCATION FOR TEACHERS:
OPENING THE PROFESSION TO WOMEN

Catharine Beecher's third major project, begun in her later years, was to recruit and train young women in the east to teach in the burgeoning western communities. She encouraged females working long hours in unsafe factories at low pay to obtain some teacher education (initially only a month-long) and go west where wages were higher and prospective husbands plentiful. She knew—even hoped—that most of the young women would soon marry, but felt a career as a homemaker was equally if not more important. Besides, a mother's childrearing techniques would be much improved after applying effective teaching and discipline strategies in the classroom.

Beecher joined Horace Mann's crusade for "common schools" (public schools), begun in the 1820s, and urged their establishment in the "uncivilized" western states in order to protect women and children and save the family. She wrote:

> We find that in one of our smallest middle states, thirty thousand adults and children are entirely without education and without schools. In one of the largest middle states, four hundred thousand adults and children are thus destitute. In one of the best educated western states, one-third of the children are without schools; while it appears, that, in the whole nation, there are a million and a half of children, and nearly as many adults, in the same deplorable ignorance, and without any means in instruction. (1835, 180)

The daughter and sister of evangelical preachers, Catharine Beecher viewed common schools as an extension of the church and saw them as places to teach Protestant religious values as well as basic skills. However, she had by this time soundly rejected Calvinism for what she considered its psychological damage, especially to children, and had become an Episcopalian. Along with Horace Mann (a Unitarian), she believed that these schools should be nonsectarian (although Protestant). Staffed by enlightened, trained teachers they would be the salvation of society's moral behavior.

With her brother-in-law Calvin Stowe and former Vermont governor William Slade, Beecher organized the Board of National Popular Education in 1847 to recruit teachers. When Slade, who considered her too domineering, took over the leadership of the board, Beecher turned her energies to establishing teacher education schools in Iowa, Illinois, and Wisconsin. In 1852, she founded the American Women's Education Association. The longest lasting of these schools was the Milwaukee Female Seminary, which later merged with Downer College and eventually became part of the University of Wisconsin-Milwaukee.

At the time Beecher began this work, most teachers were male and not well regarded. She disdained many of them as "coarse, hard, unfeeling men, too lazy or stupid" to teach children adequately and humanely (Rugoff, 186). Furthermore, men were abandoning teaching for new opportunities and better paying positions in business and industry. No paid occupation, including teaching, was considered suitable at the time for middle-class young women who were supposed to marry as soon as possible and bear many children. Beecher also believed this was women's primary role, but recognized that some, like herself, would not marry immediately if ever. Teaching, she was convinced, would be a worthwhile career for single women and excellent preparation for those who became wives, mothers, and homemakers. However, Beecher noted that changing the public's view was an uphill battle for: "[Teaching] has been looked upon as the resource of poverty, or as a drudgery suited only to inferior minds and far beneath the aims of the intelligent aspirant for fame and influence, or of the active competitor for wealth and distinction . . . this profession has never, until very recently, commanded, or secured the effort of *gifted minds*" (1829, 147). By establishing teacher-training schools, she aimed to raise the standards for teachers, improve the education of children, create more nurturing classroom environments, and elevate the career in the eyes of the public.

A product of the Victorian age, Beecher believed that females, with their modesty and nurturing dispositions, were better suited than males to teach young children the moral ways of living. Unfortunately, women teachers would also work for one-half or even one-third the pay of their male counterparts. To community leaders of the west, Beecher pointed out that a woman is "the best, as well as the cheapest guardian and teacher of childhood" (Rugoff,

188). The latter was, at least initially, perhaps the stronger reason for the acceptance of females as teachers until eventually the profession became virtually seen as "women's work."

CRITICS

In some ways, Catharine Beecher's perception of female needs and abilities was far ahead of the times. All her life she insisted that girls should receive an education equal to that of boys and that women were as intelligent as men. She never felt inferior to her accomplished brothers and was a prominent female role model for independent thinking and action. However, because she reinforced prevailing mores about a woman's place in society and opposed both the women's suffrage and abolitionist movements, she often has been criticized. Although a public figure all her adult life, she echoed her father's views against women speaking in mixed audiences, believing it harmed a woman's femininity. Her many speeches on education were read to mixed audiences by her brother Thomas or some other male relative.

Beecher was dismayed by the demands for women's right to vote, a cause in which her younger sister Isabella Beecher was greatly involved, because she felt this challenge to male supremacy was unnecessary and un-Christian. She angered her activist contemporaries by such statements as: "Heaven has appointed to one sex the superior, and to the other the subordinate station, and this without any reference to the character or conduct of either. It is therefore as much for the dignity as it is for the interest of females, in all respects to conform to the duties of this relation" (1837, 99). In other words, women would have more protection and contribute more to the nation's well-being if they stayed out of the political realm and worked at the moral center of society—the home and school. If they were unassuming and gentle, they would have much influence and power, for men would readily yield to their wishes.

Beecher's writings on domestic education were aimed at middle- and upper class females who could stay at home to raise their children and carry out homemaking activities. She seemed less interested in helping women who, for whatever reason, were forced to work outside the home in order to survive and care for their families. Thus, in modern times she has been criticized for her elitism as well as her narrow view of women's role in society. Beecher wrote primarily for the middle-class because that is the society she knew and because these were the women who, she believed, had the intelligence, time, and means to effect positive changes in morals, education, and health. She felt they would be more successful by utilizing indirect methods of persuasion and influence in the home, rather than in the contentious world of "dirty politics." According to Boydston, Kelley, and Margolis in *The Limits of Sisterhood*, in Beecher's view "submission did not mean subservience. . . . Women were to exercise power; they merely were not to be *perceived* as exercising it" (120).

Despite her lifelong assertion that women were as intelligent and capable as men, and her own forceful leadership activities, Beecher was aware that most women were dependent on husbands or male relatives for financial support and would be at great risk if they directly challenged legal and social barriers. The result could be a backlash that would harm all women and reduce further what few rights they had. She was especially fearful that their opportunities for education, which lay at the center of her life's work, would be curtailed.

Beecher also has been criticized for her autocratic behavior. Ironically, the ideal female she espoused was everything she herself was not. Far from being gentle, submissive, and home-bound, she was aggressive, overbearing, and undomesticated. While stressing in her books the need for women to promote family peace and tranquillity, she was often a meddlesome troublemaker in her own family. Beecher advocated teaching as a means for single women to gain economic independence, yet invested her own earnings into personal projects and, to the irritation of some of her siblings and their spouses, was dependent on them for shelter and other basic needs.

Not only did Catharine Beecher oppose the women's suffrage movement, but also abolitionism and the Civil War. Despite their differences of opinion, she remained close to her sister Harriet Beecher Stowe, made famous by *Uncle Tom's Cabin*. Beecher agreed that slavery was evil, but appeared not to comprehend the degree of degradation and suffering that it caused. In her *An Essay on Slavery and Abolitionism* (1837), she castigated the abolitionists for their militant tactics, and argued that both the nation and the slaves would be better served by gradual emancipation. Information and persuasion are more reasonable and effective ways of changing attitudes and behavior than violence, she maintained. Given the terrible tragedies on both sides of the Civil War and over a century of de facto subjugation of African Americans after emancipation, perhaps her position had validity.

LATER YEARS AND LASTING ACHIEVEMENTS

In 1869, with the help of her sister Harriet, Catharine Beecher revised and updated two earlier works that she put into one volume renamed *The American Woman's Home*. From age fifty-five to seventy-four, she published ten more books and wrote numerous articles for magazines, mainly on women's health and the "true profession" of homemaking. In her last year, Beecher gave a series of lectures on the "Adaptation of Woman's Education for Home Life" at Elmira (New York) College, near the home of her brother Thomas with whom she was residing. Still full of enthusiasm, she planned to make an extended tour to promote improvement in public school education.

Despite her faults, Beecher was greatly admired by friends, family, and the general public for her lively spirit and innovative ideas. She traveled the country organizing schools, writing popular books, and raising funds for her numerous endeavors. Deprived of marriage, children, and home life by the untimely death of her fiancé, Beecher created in her writings the imaginary world she had longed for, and found fulfillment in helping American middle-class women achieve it. Given her intelligence, energy, and strong personality, however, one might wonder how long she would have contentedly played the role of dutiful, submissive wife.

Catharine Esther Beecher died in 1878 at age seventy-eight and was buried in Elmira, New York. The author of twenty-five books and many more articles, she had lived a zestful and productive life. Her death was widely noted in newspapers, which stressed her far-reaching activities on behalf of education. She not only helped females advance intellectually and made public school teaching a respectable profession for women, but her widely read books elevated childrearing and homemaking into an enlightened career, at least for the middle class. Thus, women, children, and whole families across the nation benefited from Catharine Beecher's lifelong dedication to many facets of education in American society.

Excerpts from Catharine E. Beecher

In an essay entitled "The Education of Female Teachers," delivered to the American Lyceum in New York in 1835, Beecher argued that if young females were to receive education anywhere near the quality of that given males, more teachers, equipment, and books would have to be provided at public expense. Although it was flattering for men to think that girls could learn as much as boys with less qualified teachers and no library, she remarked sarcastically, such was not possible. She put forth a plan for what she considered to be a proper curriculum for educating young females for intelligent adulthood. She valued the domestic arts, but incorporated into the girls' studies the same rigorous subjects as those found in schools for male students.

The mere committing to memory of the facts contained in books, is but a small portion of education. Certain portions of time should be devoted to fitting a woman for her practical duties: such, for example, as needlework. Other pursuits are designed for the cultivation of certain mental faculties, such as *attention, perseverance,* and *accuracy.* This for example, is the influence of the study of the mathematics; while the conversation and efforts of a teacher, directed to this end, may induce habits of investigation and correct reasoning, not to be secured by any other method. Other pursuits are designed to cultivate the taste and imagination: such as rhetoric, poetry, and other branches of polite literature. Some studies are fitted to form correct moral principles, and strengthen religious obligation: such as mental and moral philosophy, the study of the evidences of Christianity, the study of the Bible, and of collateral subjects. Other studies are designed to store the mind with useful knowledge: such, for example, as geography, history, and the natural sciences. The proper selection and due proportion of these various pursuits, will have a decided influence in forming the mental habits and general character of the pupils.

Another important object in regard to female education is, the provision of suitable facilities for instruction, such as are deemed indispensable for the other sex, particularly apparatus and libraries.

While the branches now included in a course of education for females of the higher circles have increased, till nearly as much is attempted, as, were it properly taught, is demanded of young men at college, little has been done to secure a corresponding change, in regard to the necessary facilities to aid in instruction.

To teach young men properly in chemistry, natural philosophy, and other branches of science, it is deemed necessary to furnish a teacher for each separate branch, who must be prepared by a long previous course of study, who shall devote his exclusive attention to it, and who shall be furnished with apparatus at the expense of thousands of dollars; while, to aid both teachers and pupils, extensive libraries must be provided, and all at public expense.

But when the same branches are to be taught to females, one teacher is considered enough to teach a dozen such sciences, and that too without any apparatus, without any qualifying process, and without any library.

If females are to have the same branches included in their education as the other sex, ought there not to be a corresponding change to provide the means for having them properly taught; or are our sex to be complimented with the intimation that a single teacher, without preparatory education, without apparatus, and without libraries, can teach young ladies what it requires half a dozen teachers, fitted by a long course of study and furnished with every facility of books and apparatus, to teach young gentleman? We certainly are not ambitious of such compliments to the intellectual superiority of our sex (174–176).

> In this essay Beecher presented her plan for attracting unmarried women into teaching, establishing teacher-training seminaries, and providing female teachers for the thousands of schools needed in newly settled western communities. She stressed her abiding theme that the education, skills, and temperament suited for teaching were the same as those needed for motherhood; thus single educated women who dedicated a few years of their lives to the classroom would also be preparing for their even more important career as a homemaker and mother. Married women were not allowed to teach in the common (public) schools in the nineteenth century, but should a woman not marry she would still have a respectable profession that used her intelligence and talents and gave her economic independence.

When we consider the claims of the learned professions, the excitement and profits of commerce, manufactures, agriculture, and the arts; when we consider the aversion of most men to the sedentary, confining, and toilsome duties of teaching and governing young children; when we consider the scanty pittance that is allowed to the majority of teachers; and that few men will enter a business that will not support a family, when there are multitudes of other employments that will afford competence, and lead to wealth; it is chimerical to hope that the supply of such immense deficiencies in our national education is to come chiefly from that sex. It is woman, fitted by disposition, and habits, and circumstances, for such duties, who, to a very wide extent, must aid in educating the childhood and youth of this nation; and therefore it is, that females must be trained and educated for this employment. And, most happily, it is true, that the education necessary to fit a woman to be a teacher, is exactly the one that best fits her for that domestic relation she is primarily designed to fill.

But how is this vast undertaking to be accomplished? How can such a multitude of female teachers as are needed, be secured and fitted for such duties? The following will show how it *can* be done, if those most interested and obligated shall only *will* to have it done.

Men of patriotism and benevolence can commence by endowing two or three seminaries for female teachers in the most important stations in the nation, while to each of these seminaries shall be attached a model school, supported by the children of the place where it is located. In these seminaries can be collected those who have the highest estimate of the value of moral and religious influence, and the most talents and experience for both intellectual and moral education.

When these teachers shall have succeeded in training classes of teachers on the best system their united wisdom can devise, there will be instructors prepared for other seminaries for teachers, to be organized and conducted on the same plan; and thus a regular and systematic course of education can be disseminated through the nation.

Meantime, proper efforts being made by means of the press, the pulpit, and influential men employed as agents for this object, the interest of the whole nation can be aroused, and every benevolent and every pious female in the nation, who has the time and qualifications necessary, can be enlisted to consecrate at least a certain number of years to this object. There is not a village in this nation that cannot furnish its one, two, three, and in some cases ten or twenty, laborers for this field.

And, as a system of right moral and religious education gains its appropriate influence, as women are more and more educated to understand and value the importance of their influence in society, and their peculiar duties, more young females will pursue their education with the expectation that, unless paramount private duties forbid, they are to employ their time and talents in the duties of a teacher, until they assume the responsibilities of domestic life. Females will cease to feel that they are educated just to enjoy themselves in future life, and realize the obligations imposed by Heaven to live to do good. And, when females are educated as they ought to be, every woman at the close of her school education, will be well qualified to act as a teacher (1835, 183–185).

> Two of Catharine Beecher's early books on homemaking, reprinted numerous times, helped to make her one of America's best-known women. In an updated version of these two works, renamed *The American Woman's Home* (1869) and expanded in collaboration with her sister Harriet Beecher Stowe, Catharine Beecher set forth a major theme, stressed repeatedly in subsequent writings, that the labor women do in the home has inestimable value and should receive the same respect as work done by men in the larger world. The book gave practical, sensible, specific advice on an amazing array of topics related to domestic duties—few of which Catharine had any direct experience with beyond a few years helping to raise younger siblings and many years observing friends and relatives.

Any discussion of the equality of the sexes, as to intellectual capacity, seems frivolous and useless, both because it can never be decided, and because there would be no possible advantage in the decision. But one topic, which is often drawn into this discussion, is of far more consequence; and that is, the relative importance and difficulty of the duties a woman is called to perform.

It is generally assumed, and almost as generally conceded, that a housekeeper's business and cares are contracted and trivial; and that the proper discharge of her duties demands far less expansion of mind and vigor of intellect than the pursuits of the other sex. This idea has prevailed because women, as a mass, have never been educated with reference to their most important duties; while that portion of their employments which is of least value has been regarded as the chief, if not the sole, concern of a woman. The covering of the body, the convenience of residences, and the gratification of the appetite, have been too much regarded as the chief objects on which her intellectual powers are to be exercised.

But as society gradually shakes off the remnants of barbarism and the intellectual and moral interests of man rise, in estimation, above the merely sensual, a truer estimate is formed of woman's duties, and of the measure of intellect requisite for the proper discharge of them. Let any man of sense and discernment become the member of a large household, in which a well-educated and pious woman is endeavoring systematically to discharge her multiform duties; let him fully comprehend all her cares, difficulties, and perplexities; and it is probable he would coincide in the opinion that no statesman, at the head of a nation's affairs, had more frequent calls for wisdom, firmness, tact, discrimination, prudence, and versatility of talent, than such a woman. . . .

Surely, it is a pernicious and mistaken idea, that the duties which tax a woman's mind are petty, trivial, or unworthy of the highest grade of intellect and moral worth. . . . She ought to feel that her station and responsibilities in the great drama of life are second to none, either as viewed by her Maker, or in the estimation of all minds whose judgement is most worthy of respect (1869, 220–222).

> Beecher also believed that children of both sexes should be taught the same skills, and that domestic arts should not be seen as belonging only to females. Not only would each learn to appreciate the value of these responsibilities, but would be better able to fend for themselves as adults if they were skilled in the duties normally assigned to the opposite sex as well as their own.

There are some mothers who take pains to teach their boys most of the domestic arts which their sisters learn. The writer has seen boys mending their own garments and aiding their mother or sisters in the kitchen, with great skill and adroitness; and, at an early age, they usually very much relish joining in such occupations. The sons of such mothers, in their college life, or in roaming about the world, or in nursing a sick wife or infant, find occasion to bless the forethought and kindness which prepared them for such emergencies . . . a man never appears in a more interesting attitude than when, by skill in such matters, he can save a mother or wife from care and suffering. The more a boy is taught to use his hands, in every variety of domestic employment, the more his faculties, both of mind and body, are developed; for mechanical pursuits exercise the intellect as well as the hands (1869, 229).

It is equally important that young girls should be taught to do some species of handicraft that generally is done by men, and especially with reference to the frequent emigration to new territories where well-trained mechanics are scarce. To hang wallpaper, repair locks, glaze windows, and mend various household articles, requires a skill in the use of tools which every young girl should acquire. If she never has any occasion to apply this knowledge and skill by her own hands, she will often find it needful in directing and superintending incompetent workmen (1869, 229–230).

> Discussed next are suggestions for disciplining children that sound surprisingly modern in their concern for preserving self-esteem and promoting happiness.

First: Avoid, as much as possible, the multiplication of rules and absolute commands. Instead of this, take the attitude of advisers. "My child, this is improper, I wish you would remember not to do it." This mode of address answers for all the little acts of heedlessness, awkwardness, or ill-manners so frequently occurring with children. There are cases, when direct and distinct commands are needful; and in such cases, a penalty for disobedience should be as steady and sure as the laws of nature. Where such steadiness and certainty of penalty attend disobedience, children no more think of disobeying than they do of putting their fingers into a burning candle.

The next maxim is, Govern by rewards more than by penalties. Such faults as willful disobedience, lying, dishonesty, and indecent or profane language, should be punished with severe penalties, after a child has been fully instructed in the evil of such practices. But all the constantly recurring faults of the nursery, such as ill-humor, quarreling, carelessness, and ill-manners, may, in a great many cases, be regulated by gentle and kind remonstrances, and by the offer of some reward for persevering efforts to form a good habit. It is very injurious and degrading to any mind to be kept under the constant fear of penalties. *Love* and *hope* are the principles that should be mainly relied on, in forming the habits of childhood.

Another maxim, and perhaps the most difficult, is, Do not govern by the aid of severe and angry tones. . . . The writer has been in some families where the most efficient and steady government has been sustained without the use of a cross or angry tone; and in others, where a far less efficient discipline was kept up, by frequent severe rebukes and angry remonstrances. In the first case, the children followed the example set them, and seldom used severe tones to each other; in the latter, the method employed by the parents was imitated by the children, and cross words and angry tones resounded from morning till night, in every portion of the household.

Another important maxim is, Try to keep children in a happy state of mind. Every one knows, by experience, that it is easier to do right and submit to rule when cheerful and happy, than when irritated. This is peculiarly true of children; and a wise mother, when she finds her child fretful and impatient, and thus constantly doing wrong, will often remedy the whole difficulty, by telling some amusing story, or by getting the child engaged in some amusing sport. This strongly shows the importance of learning to govern children without the employment of angry tones, which always produce irritation.

Children of active, heedless temperament, or those who are odd, awkward, or unsuitable in their remarks and deportment, are often essentially injured by a want of patience and self-control in those who govern them. Such children often possess a morbid sensibility which they strive to conceal, or a desire of love and approbation, which preys like a famine on the soul. And yet, they become objects of ridicule and rebuke to almost every member of the family, until their sensibilities are tortured into obtuseness or misanthropy. Such children, above all others, need tenderness and sympathy. A thousand instances of mistake or forgetfulness should be passed over in silence, while opportunities for commendation and encouragement should be diligently sought (1869, 282–284).

REFERENCES

Beecher, C. E. (1829). "Suggestions respecting improvements in education." In Goodsell, W. (1931). *Pioneers of women's education in the United States: Emma Willard, Catharine Beecher, Mary Lyon.* New York: McGraw-Hill.

———. (1835). "An essay on the education of female teachers." In Goodsell, W. (1931). *Pioneers of women's education in the United States: Emma Willard, Catharine Beecher, Mary Lyon.* New York: McGraw-Hill.

———. (1837). *An essay on slavery and abolitionism, with reference to the duty of American females.* Philadelphia: Henry Perkins.

———. (1841). *A treatise on domestic economy for the use of young ladies at home and at school.* New York: Harper & Brothers.

————. (1846). *Miss Beecher's domestic receipt book.* New York: Harper & Brothers.

————. (1856). "Letters to the people on health and happiness." In Goodsell, W. (1931). *Pioneers of women's education in the United States: Emma Willard, Catharine Beecher, Mary Lyon.* New York: McGraw-Hill.

————. (1869). With Harriet Beecher Stowe. *The American woman's home, or the principles of domestic science.* New York: J. B. Ford.

————. (1873). *Miss Beecher's housekeeper and healthkeeper.* New York: Harper & Brothers.

Boydston, J., Kelley, M., & Margolis, A. (1988). *The limits of sisterhood: The Beecher sisters on women's rights and woman's sphere.* Chapel Hill: University of North Carolina Press.

Rugoff, M. (1981). *The Beechers: An American family in the nineteenth century.* New York: Harper & Row.

Sklar, K. K. (1973). *Catharine Beecher: A study in domesticity.* New Haven, CT: Yale University Press.

SELECTED OTHER WORKS BY CATHARINE BEECHER

The true remedy for the wrongs of women. (1851). Boston: Phillips, Sampson.

Common sense applied to religion, or the Bible and the people. (1856). New York: Harper & Brothers.

Physiology and calisthenics for school and families (1856). New York: Harper & Brothers.

Woman suffrage and woman's profession. (1871). Hartford, CT: Brown & Gross.

Educational reminiscences and suggestions. (1874). New York: J. B. Ford.

SELECTED OTHER WORKS ABOUT CATHARINE BEECHER

Cross, B. (Ed.). (1965). *The educated woman in America: Selected writings of Catharine Beecher, Margaret Fuller, Cary Thomas.* New York: Teachers College Press.

Harveson, M. E. (1932). *Catharine Beecher, pioneer educator.* Philadelphia: University of Pennsylvania Press. (Reprint, New York: Arno Press, 1969).

Woody, T. (1929). *A history of women's education in the United States* (Vol. I). New York: Science Press. (Reprint, New York: Octagon Books, Farrar, Straus & Giroux, 1974).

2

Elizabeth Palmer Peabody: Educating Young Children

In today's schools a determined effort is being made to meet differing student needs, encourage creativity and individual talents, and promote cooperative, caring behaviors. This was done quite successfully over one hundred years ago in the innovation called *kindergartens*.

The kindergarten movement owes its acceptance and rapid growth in America to the untiring efforts of Elizabeth Palmer Peabody. She is credited with opening the first English-speaking kindergarten in this country, based initially on the philosophy of the German educator and founder of kindergartens, Friedrich Froebel.

Enthralled by Froebel's approach to early education, Peabody dedicated her last thirty years promoting kindergartens in America through writing, lecturing, opening schools, training teachers, and inspiring followers. She was revered as the quintessential educator, affectionately caricatured by Henry James as "Miss Birdseye" in *The Bostonians*, and esteemed by the many whom she had generously, although sometimes overzealously, aided in personal and professional ways. Above all, she was an energetic optimist who believed in human goodness and never despaired despite un-reached goals, financial insecurity, and public or private criticism.

EARLY YEARS

Elizabeth Peabody was born in Billerica, Massachusetts, in 1804, the eldest of seven children. She was primed to be an educator from an early age. Besides the fact that teaching was one of the few oc-cupations open to bright, middle-class females, she was highly in-fluenced by her mother, a self-educated, intelligent woman who in her home ran a successful school for girls with a rigorous curricu-lum. Elizabeth learned Latin from her dentist father who also had been a teacher. In 1820, at age sixteen, she moved with her parents and younger siblings to Lancaster, Massachusetts, where she took over her mother's school. Among the pupils were her sisters Mary (who later married Horace Mann, the father of the "common school" movement) and Sophia (who married the writer Nathaniel Hawthorne).

Elizabeth was ten years old when she first heard a sermon by the Unitarian minister, William Ellery Channing. Her mother embraced this liberal religion and encouraged her daughter to be an indepen-dent thinker and questioner. At age eighteen, Elizabeth went to Boston to live on her own and again was entranced by Channing's theology. She volunteered to record by hand his sermons, public talks, group discussions, and personal conversations, which years later she used for her book, *Reminiscences of the Reverend William E. Channing* (1880). Along with Friedrich Froebel, the founder of kin-dergartens in Germany, Channing was one of the major influences on Peabody's educational philosophy.

INTELLECTUAL LIFE AND
EARLY TEACHING EXPERIENCES

For the next twenty years, Elizabeth Peabody taught in her own schools or in others, wrote articles and books on education, history and religion, and became known in Boston as a woman of high in-tellect and knowledge. She read prodigiously, studied many lan-guages, translated works from French, German, Greek, and Italian, gave numerous "conversations" about ancient history to women in private homes (women were barred by custom from giving public lectures), and was one of the few women members of the elite Transcendental Club. Her nephew claimed her to be the most learned woman in the world, and her brother-in-law, Horace Mann, fondly called her "Miss Thesaura." However, because Peabody's later efforts concerned the education of young children, an endeavor not highly regarded by scholars, historians have largely ignored her intellectual abilities and contributions, despite her close ties to the leading religious, philosophic, and literary leaders of her day.

The goal of education, Channing stressed to Peabody, was moral and intellectual freedom, requiring free speech, free inquiry, respect for all persons, and belief in human virtue. Elizabeth was especially impressed by his love for children's innocence and spontaneity. He rejected the belief that young minds and actions should be molded by adults, arguing that each child was a unique person, whose nature should be carefully studied and reverently dealt with. In contrast to prevailing school practices, Channing maintained that dominating children was the opposite of education, for it ignored their own consciousness and did not lead them to self-understanding and self-direction.

In 1832, Elizabeth, with her sister Mary, opened a school and rented living quarters in a boarding house in Brookline, Massachusetts. Also living there was Horace Mann, who, as State Representative, was highly involved in improving conditions for prisoners and the mentally ill. Both sisters were attracted to Mann, who was mourning the recent death of his young wife, and for several years each separately consoled him through conversations and correspondence. It was quiet, conventional Mary, however, who eventually won his heart.

Because of the Peabody sisters' school efforts, Mann soon became interested in education himself. He served as Massachusetts' first Secretary of Education (a lowly, poorly paid position), and spent much of his life promoting the idea of free "common schools," financed by public taxation, that would benefit children from all strata of society. In his last years, he was president of Antioch College, a radical school in Yellow Springs, Ohio, that admitted women students on an equal basis with men.

In 1834, at age thirty, Elizabeth Peabody became the assistant to A. Bronson Alcott (father of Louisa May Alcott) in his small experimental school in an old Masonic temple in Boston. To save expenses, Elizabeth lived with the family, who named their daughter Elizabeth (immortalized as Beth in *Little Women*) after her. At first, Peabody was impressed by Alcott's long, introspective discussions with young children about all aspects of life. She faithfully recorded one month's conversations and in 1835 published them in a book called *Record of a School* which sold well and received wide notice.

Soon, however, she began to doubt the wisdom of these inner probings, feeling them an invasion of privacy and mentally unhealthy. Although she liked Alcott's attempt to bring out the innate knowledge of children rather than pour in facts, she wanted more physical activity and less passive pondering. When in 1836 Alcott published Peabody's second recordings of his teaching, called *Conversations with Children on the Gospels*, which revealed frank discussions about birth and circumcision, Boston was outraged and the school soon closed. Humiliated by the publicity and angered by Alcott's domineering manner and inability to pay her salary, Elizabeth moved to Salem to live with her parents.

On reading her earlier work *Record of a School*, Ralph Waldo Emerson, whom she had known in their youth, invited her to join the Transcendental Club, which included the leading intelligentsia of Boston. In 1840, as the nation was slowly emerging from a severe depression, Peabody opened a foreign language bookshop and library in her West Street home in Boston. For ten years it was the gathering place for such thinkers as Emerson, Margaret Fuller, George Ripley, James Freeman Clarke, Orestes Brownson, Jones Very, and Theodore Parker. She volunteered her shop for Fuller's "conversations" and was the publisher of the Transcendentalist organ, *The Dial*, for which she wrote articles and served as editor for two years. She also produced one issue of a journal called *Aesthetic Papers* in 1849 with articles by Emerson, Thoreau, Hawthorne, and other prominent writers.

KINDERGARTENS IN AMERICA

After closing the shop in 1850, Peabody turned again to education. When she was fifty-five years old, she met political emigré Margarethe Schurz, who ran a small German-speaking kindergarten in Watertown, Wisconsin. Trained by Friedrich Froebel, who originated kindergartens in Germany, Schurz urged Peabody to read Froebel's large book, later translated into English as *The Education of Man* (1896). His philosophy affirmed Peabody's own teaching experiences and view of children's moral nature.

With the help of her sister Mary Mann, who had started a school for young children after the death of her husband Horace Mann, Peabody opened the first English-speaking kindergarten in America on Pinckney Street in Boston. Already respected as an innovative educator, she was able to attract children from high-status families, and the school was an instant success. Together, the sisters wrote several books and worked the rest of their lives (although not always harmoniously) in opening schools, training teachers, and promoting early childhood education.

The kindergarten movement was welcomed by the upper and middle classes and spread rapidly, for childhood was at last being viewed as a unique stage of development. Children were not just small adults, but differed in behavior, language, and thought, and needed special care and attention so they would grow into upright, social, civil human beings. Increasingly, raising children was seen as women's major responsibility, at a time when industrialization was removing the father from the home during much of the day. The kindergarten, then, became an extension of the home and was based as much as possible on mother love.

Soon, however, Peabody grew dissatisfied with the school, which she felt stressed the mental growth of children at the expense of physical, artistic, and spiritual development. Feeling the need to learn more, she gave a series of history lectures to earn money, and at age sixty-two went to Europe to visit German kindergartens first-hand. Froebel had died a few years earlier, but many of the teachers he had trained welcomed her into their classrooms and enthusiastically shared their knowledge, educational philosophy, and teaching strategies.

On her return to the United States, Peabody threw herself into promoting such schools across America, convinced that they were the key to teaching a true democracy, setting children on the path to freedom, creativity, self-respect, and intellectual exploration. She published many articles and books that discussed the purpose and methods of kindergartens and their importance in developing happy, healthy children and responsible citizens. This dedicated involvement with young children, however, doomed her reputation as a scholar. Although historians and others may not view the promotion of kindergartens as an intellectual endeavor, Peabody be-lieved it to be the culmination of a lifetime of research, reflection, writings, and social action.

KINDERGARTEN PHILOSOPHY

The main aim of a Froebel kindergarten was to help children grow organically, with the help of a well-trained "gardener." Wrote Peabody in *Lectures in the Training Schools for Kindergartners* (1906): "A kindergarten means a guarded company of children, who are to be treated as a gardener treats his plants; that is, in the first place, studied to see what they are, and what conditions they require for the fullest and most beautiful growth. . . . It is because they are liv-ing organisms that they are to be *cultivated*—not *drilled* (which is a process only appropriate to insensate stone)" (4–5). In this ap-proach, children should not be dominated and manipulated, nor left alone without guidance: How would a garden of flowers fare, to be planted, and then left to grow with so little scientific care taken by the gardener, as is bestowed upon children between one and five years old? (1906, 4). However, she believed, children should also not be pampered, but guided to develop *"common* sense and *common* conscience with a reasonable self respect . . . their idiosyncrasies being left free to play on the surface and give variety and piquancy to life, freedom and dignity to the individual" (1906, 79).

Essential to the success of every kindergarten teacher was the belief in the goodness of children. In contrast to the doctrine still prevalent at the time, Peabody believed that children were born good, not sinful. She repudiated the use of punishment and the at-tempt to break a child's will. Instead, she advocated bringing the child's desires and behavior into harmony with others through love, gentleness, and patience and talking to children as equals rather than exercising authority.

Teacher Characteristics

Wrote Elizabeth Peabody, "Those persons who feel that educa-tion is wearisome work have not learned the secret of it. I have never seen a good [kindergarten teacher] who was not as fond of the work as a painter of his painting, a sculptor of his modeling" (1906, 88). Kindergarten teaching, she maintained, requires more ability, not less, than teaching older students, for such teachers are responsible for the early formation of understanding. This requires not only profound insight into how children at that age learn but also a knowledge of how children think and feel, which can only be obtained by close observation and study. Instead of looking down on children as lesser beings, she insisted, kindergarten teachers should "humbly look up to the innocent soul" of each child. An affectionate nature was thus essential to a good kindergarten teacher for "love is the truest quickener of industry" (1906, 14, 77).

Although kindergartens were started in Germany by a man, and educators today stress the need for male teachers in early childhood education, Peabody believed that the skills needed by kindergarten teachers were expressly suited to females: "To be a [kindergarten teacher] is the perfect development of womanliness—a working with God at the very fountain of artistic and intellectual power and moral character. It is therefore the highest finish that can be given to a woman's education" (1906, 13).

Methods of Teaching

The methods used in Peabody's kindergartens, radical for the time, were play, art, music, reflective discussion, physical exercise, observation, classification by names—but not reading. Peabody believed that reading, when taught too soon, was injurious, producing a habit of mind that dropped "a veil between the observer and nature, preventing all freshness of thought, and destroying the mind's elasticity and *originality*" (1906, 146). All school activities should be aimed at helping children achieve success because unsuccessful efforts were so discouraging as to prevent them from wanting to work further. Guidance by the teacher should be tentative and respectful of the child's will, with care taken not to choke spontaneity.

Education, stated Peabody, was primarily moral and spiritual, by example rather than precept. The major tasks of a teacher were to produce tender, respectful courtesy in the pupils towards each other, aiding them to discover and develop their personal strengths and goals. Like Channing and Froebel, she believed each person to be a unique organism, divinely created with special attributes, who will unfold according to an internal law if properly guided and lovingly cared for. Her Romantic idealism, which grew out of nineteenth-century Unitarian and Transcendentalist beliefs, was perfectly attuned to the early childhood educational philosophy that repudiated the stultifying cruel practices of both public and private schools. Kindergartens, as she envisioned them, were humane, deeply spiritual, joyous, and liberating.

A kindergarten teacher, said Peabody, can motivate children to work at something new by starting with things they can accomplish. When they are pleased with the effect, they will want to repeat it, and will proudly show others what they have done. The teacher should give them the opportunity to put their actions into words, to talk about whatever they do, as this "raises it from mere mechanical into intellectual work" (1906, 86). In all their activities, from playing ball to doing arithmetic, children should be encouraged to discuss what they do, explain their choices and reasons, observe the properties and relations of things, and reflect on these observations according to their own understanding and viewpoint.

In Peabody's kindergartens, a teacher began each day with songs that the children selected and a few words of her own. This was followed by free conversation where each child had the opportunity to say whatever was uppermost in her or his mind. The teacher's role was to listen attentively to whatever was said, no matter how trivial, and help the children turn each comment into a reflection that promoted moral, social, or intellectual growth. Peabody felt this free conversation was the most important part of the day.

The kindergarten teacher, she emphasized, needs to know how to converse with children and play with them, rather than coercing them into doing her will, no matter how kindly. Play, she believed, was the most genuine and intense aspect of a child's life, and teachers need to respect the child's desires and not hinder their free will, movement, or creativity: "The fanciful plays of the kindergarten, whether sedentary or moving, cultivate the imagination, the understanding, and the physical powers in harmony, and more than this, they cultivate the heart and conscience because . . . everything they make is intended for others" (1906, 211).

The role of the teacher is to bring out the child's inner essence. Instead of telling children how to do things, which they merely imitate, or telling them what to learn or see, the teacher prepares the environment, like a gardener tilling the soil, so that the children can discover for themselves. Their individual, innate natures can thus develop at their own pace and in their own way. The teacher can introduce scientific facts, like light and color, to enhance the children's discovery, but through talk they make their own observations about the meaning and significance of the facts, from their own childish perspectives.

Methods of Discipline

The normal method of controlling behavior in most schools at the time was corporal punishment, often harshly administered. Based on the Calvinist belief in innate depravity, physical punishment was deemed necessary to conquer the children's sinful natures. Peabody, however, believed that children were born moral, not sinful. The way to develop character, she stressed, was through patience, gentleness, and affection. Kindergarten teachers must have a love "that involves patience, that can stand the manifestation of ugly temper, and perverse will, and never lose sight of the embryo angel that wears for the moment the devilish mask. In children, evil is actual, but always superficial and temporary, if the educator does not become party to it by losing her temper and idea" (1906, 15). One should never embarrass a child in front of others, she maintained, nor vent one's authority, but rather treat children as friends and equals. If a child becomes rude or violent while playing, he or she should be removed and made to stand in a corner alone, or even outside the room, until the child expresses a desire to rejoin classmates and exhibits a more considerate and pleasant attitude. In the early years, she continued: "The child should be treated with unvarying tenderness and consideration, without having his senses pampered into morbid excess by over-indulgence, but above all things, never wounding nor frightening his heart, nor repressing the simple and healthy expression of his feelings and thoughts" (1906, 59–60).

OTHER CONTRIBUTIONS

Besides her prodigious work promoting kindergartens, Peabody was involved in many social causes. Although she accepted the middle-class view of women as mainly nurturers (kindergartens being an extension of home and mother love), she herself was the epitome of a dedicated professional. A writer, thinker, teacher, business woman, and social action leader, she never doubted the intellectual abilities of women, was on equal terms with Boston's male intelligentsia, and promoted female education throughout her lifetime. She did, however, cringe at women speaking to mixed audiences, particularly on matters pertaining to the body, and criticized other women for doing so.

From early on, Peabody was involved in the antislavery movement. For a short while, she taught at a progressive school run by abolitionists Theodore Weld and his wife Angelina Grimke, and from her West Street bookshop she published an Emancipation pamphlet written by William Ellery Channing. Peabody also helped establish a school for African-American orphans in Washington, DC, where Mary Mann's niece, Maria Mann, was a teacher.

In her later years, Peabody championed the cause of Native Americans, especially their rights to education and the retention of tribal ways. She was also active to the end in the temperance movement, the treatment of prisoners and the insane, and world peace.

CRITICS

Like other female activists, Peabody was criticized for being "unfeminine" and not knowing her place in society. To earn her living, she dared to give lectures to women on history and current issues, was a businesswoman who owned a bookstore that was a meeting place for leading intellectuals, and self-confidently strode into every reform movement of the day, certain that she could make a difference.

She was condemned by many for her abolitionist statements, for publishing the antislavery tract, and for giving aid to a school for Black orphans after the Civil War. Her efforts to provide education for Native Americans without their giving up tribal ways was also criticized in some circles. Unfortunately, according to some biographers, Peabody was the victim of a con artist, "Princess Winnemucca," who bilked her out of a sizable donation collected for a school that was never built. This, however, is disputed by other researchers. In any case, Peabody's concern for improving life on the reservation was genuine and her work to publicize the Indians' economic plight was admirable.

Although she was devoutly religious and incorporated spiritual ideas into her kindergarten philosophy and books and articles, Peabody was assailed by conservative Christians who considered her beliefs anathema. She was a disciple of William Ellery

Channing, a leader in the liberal Unitarian denomination that broke away from Congregationalism in Boston. Her involvement in the Transcendentalist movement, along with Emerson, Fuller, Thoreau, and other radical thinkers of the day, plus her assertiveness and assumption of equality in matters of the intellect, were too much for many critics, both men and women, to bear.

Finally, there were those who objected to her educational philosophy. Much of Boston society was outraged by her early publication of Bronson Alcott's conversations with children on matters of sex and religion. Later, the kindergarten movement was more widely accepted and praised, but detractors deplored the "waste" of time and money on schools for young children, especially girls, where the curriculum centered around play, art, music, nature walks, and conversations initiated by the pupils. Also, her methods of discipline were considered too "soft." Young children, her critics maintained, needed to be controlled instead of coddled. Sparing the rod merely set them up to be irresponsible, self-indulgent adults.

LATER YEARS AND LASTING ACHIEVEMENTS

In addition to her many articles and speeches, Peabody founded in 1873 a monthly journal, *Kindergarten Messenger*, that was dedicated to helping teachers understand and implement the Froebel philosophy. She was seventy-three years old. Five years later the publication was joined with another and became *Kindergarten Messenger and The New Education*. In 1873, Peabody convinced the St. Louis School Board to add kindergartens to their public school system, the first in the nation to do so. She also organized and served as the honorary first president of the American Froebel Union. The rest of her years were spent in ceaseless activity promoting kindergartens across the land, giving lectures, training teachers, and raising money.

In the late 1800s, Peabody was a popular lecturer in the Concord School of Philosophy begun by A. Bronson Alcott, with whom she was reconciled. She died in 1894 at age ninety. Her grave is in Concord's Sleepy Hollow Cemetery, along with her friends Emerson, Thoreau, the Alcotts, and her brother-in-law Nathaniel Hawthorne. In death as in life she was welcomed in good company.

Two years later, the Elizabeth Peabody House was opened in Boston as a settlement house and memorial to her energetic dedication to many social causes. Her tombstone reads: "A teacher of three generations of children and the founder of Kindergartens in America. Every humane cause had her sympathy and many her active aid."

Excerpts from Elizabeth Palmer Peabody

In her late fifties, Elizabeth Peabody became entranced with Friedrich Froebel's ideas about early childhood education. With her sister Mary Mann she established in Boston in 1860 the first English-speaking kindergarten in America. Several years later, Peabody spent fifteen months visiting Froebel kindergartens, or "gardens of children," in Germany to observe the methods firsthand. She spent her remaining years helping to establish such classrooms across the country. *Guide to the Kindergarten and Intermediate Class* (1877) was an influential textbook for explaining the philosophy and training of teachers.

What is a Kindergarten? . . . It is not the old-fashioned infant-school. That was a narrow institution, comparatively; the object being . . . to take the children of poor laborers, and keep them out of the fire and the streets, while their mothers went to their necessary labor. Very good things, indeed, in their way. Their principle of discipline was to circumvent the wills of children, in every way that would enable their teachers to keep them within bounds, and quiet. It was certainly better that they should learn to sing *by rote* the Creed and the "definitions" of scientific terms, and such like, than to learn the profanity and obscenity of the streets, which was the alternative. But no mother who wished for anything which might be called the *development* of her child would think of putting it into an infant-school, especially if she lived in the country . . . where any "old grey stone" would altogether surpass, as a standpoint, the bench of the highest class of an infant school (1877, 9).

Kindergarten means a garden of children, and Froebel, the inventor of it, or rather, as he would prefer to express it, *the discoverer of the method of Nature,* meant to symbolize by the name the spirit and plan of treatment. How does the gardener treat his plants? He studies their individual natures, and puts them into such circumstances of soil and atmosphere as enable them to grow, flower, and bring forth fruit—also to renew their manifestation year after year. He does not expect to succeed unless he learns all their wants, and the circumstances in which these wants will be supplied, and all their possibilities of beauty and use, and the means of giving them opportunity to be perfected. On the other hand, while he knows that they must not be forced against their individual natures, he does not leave them to grow wild, but prunes redundancies, removes destructive worms and bugs from their leaves and stems, and weeds from their vicinity—carefully watching to learn what peculiar insects affect what particular plants, and how the former can be destroyed without injuring the vitality of the latter. After all the most careful gardener can do, he knows that the form of the plant is predetermined in the germ or seed, and that the inward tendency must concur with a multitude of influences (1877, 10). . . .

In the Kindergarten, *children* are treated on an analogous plan. It presupposes gardeners of the mind, who are quite aware that they have as little power to override the characteristic individuality of a child, or to predetermine this characteristic, as the gardener of plants to say that a lily shall be a rose...yet they must feel responsible, after all, for the perfection of the development, in so far as removing every impediment, preserving every condition, and pruning every redundance (1877, 11). . . .

It was Froebel's wisdom to accept the natural activity of childhood as a hint of the Divine Providence, and to utilize its spontaneous play for education. And it is this which takes away from his system that element of baneful antagonism which school discipline is so apt to excite, and which it is such a misfortune should ever be excited between the young and old. Nothing is worse for the soul, at any period of life, than to be put upon self-defense; for humility is the condition of the growth of mind as well as morals, and ensures that natural self-respect shall not degenerate into a petty willfulness and self-assertion. The divine impulse of activity in children should not be directly opposed, but accepted and guided into beautiful production, according to the laws of creative order, which the adult has studied out in nature, and genially presents in *playing* with the child (1877, 35–36).

> Peabody stressed the importance of educating teachers by direct experience in the philosophy and methods of kindergarten teaching. Although today we recognize the need for male teachers in preschools and early grades, and the originator of kindergartens was a man, Peabody saw such teaching to be an attractive extension of motherhood. She not only wanted to

give women a career option, but to break away from the typical male instructors of the time who meted out harsh discipline.
Females, she reasoned, would be much more nurturing, gentle,
and compassionate.

But such playing is a great art, and founded on the deepest science of nature, within and without; and therefore Froebel never
established a Kindergarten without previously preparing Kindergartners [the name Peabody used for the teachers] by a normal
training, which his faithful disciples have scrupulously kept up. . . .
Hundreds of pupils of these normal classes have proved, that any
fairly gifted, well-educated, genial-tempered young woman, who
will devote a reasonable time to training for it, can become a competent Kindergartner.

Nothing short of this will do; for none of the manuals which have
been written to guide already trained experts, can supply the place
of the living teacher. Written words will not describe the find gra-
dations of the work, or give an idea of the conversation which is
to be constantly had with the children. It would be less absurd to
suppose that a person could learn to make watches by reading a
description of the manufacture in an encyclopedia, than to suppose
a person could learn to educate children by mere formulas.

Indeed, it is *infinitely* less absurd. For a child is not finite mass
to be molded, or a blank paper to be written upon, at another's will.
It is a living subject, whose own cooperation—or at least willingness—is to be conciliated and made instrumental to the end in view.
Would a Cremona violin be put into the hands of a person ignorant of music, to be tuned and made to discourse divine harmo-
nies? . . . Looking at children's first schools, it would seem that
anybody is thought skillful enough to begin a child's education! It
takes a long apprenticeship to learn to play on the instrument with
seven strings, in order to bring out music. But it is stupidly thought
that anybody can play on the greater instrument, whose strings
thrill with pleasure or pain, and discourse good or evil, as they are
touched wisely or unwisely! (1877, 36–37).

Peabody was especially concerned about instituting new methods of discipline, which replaced fault-finding and punishment
with encouragement and sympathetic understanding. Teachers should not make too much of misbehavior, she urged, and
should accept the first indication the child wants to do what
is right. Wrongdoing in young children is a superficial thing,

and children are grateful and more respectful when an adult
has listened courteously and forgiven their faults.

Teachers often do great harm, with the best intentions, to finely
strung moral organizations. Encouragement to good should altogether predominate over warning and fault-finding. It is often
better, instead of blaming a child for short-coming, or even wrongdoing, to pity and sympathize, and, in a hopeful voice, speak of it
as something which the child did not mean to do, or at least was
sorry for as soon as done: suggesting at the same time, perhaps,
how it can be avoided another time. Above all things, an invariable
rule in moral education is not to throw a child upon self-defense.
The movement towards defending one's self and making excuses,
is worse than almost any act of overt wrong. Let the teacher always
appear as the friend who is saving or helping the child out of evil,
rather than as the accuser, judge, or executioner. Another principle
should be, not to confound or put upon the same level the tres-
passes against the by-laws of the Kindergarten, made for the
teacher's convenience, and those against the moral laws of the
universe. . . . Natural conscience always suffers when artificial
duties are imposed (1877, 56).

> Peabody continued this theme of disciplining with love and re-
> spect in *Lectures in the Training Schools for Kindergartners* (1906),
> which was directed at prospective kindergarten teachers.

A child cannot be *just* unless he is *loving*, nor attain the freedom
of moral dignity unless he asserts himself; and there is no way to
nurture this self-respect except to express respect to him, by being
as courteous to him as you are to any adult, always asking him to
explain himself and his own motives, when he seems to be in the
wrong, before you condemn him (185–186).

The one fatal thing is to wound the child's heart. It is better to
give up the point of controlling its will to righteousness for the
moment, than to do that (1906, 64).

> On her long trip to Europe, Peabody was extremely impressed
> with the kindergarten teachers in Germany who had received
> their training directly from Froebel. Although her own kinder-
> garten in Boston was well received by the children and their
> parents, she felt it was not fulfilling the philosophy of a Froebel

kindergarten. Her observations in the German schools helped
her to understand more fully how early childhood education
should be conducted.

One of the pleasantest observations that I made of the kindergartens of Germany . . . was the happy absorption of the teachers in
the children; their sympathy with them; the utter companionship
between them. I never saw a punishment; I never heard a Don't (or
its German equivalent); but when anything went wrong, there was
always a pause, and sometimes questions were asked; and all
seemed to wait till the inward guide had been brought out into
consciousness (whether the thing in hand was social action or artistic work). . . . [The kindergartner] should present order to the
mind, by her genial questioning and conversation over the work in
hand, rather than exert an arbitrary power which might stimulate
the reaction of obstinacy or the subterfuges of cunning. To *govern*
is not the whole thing. The question is *how* we govern; whether we
so govern as to make a cringing slave, a cunning hypocrite, or an
intelligent, law-abiding, self-respecting, *willing* servant of God. I
have seen a magnetic teacher produce a marvelous obedience, and
apparent order, by his imposing presence and keen satire. He imag-
ined that he governed by moral power; but as soon as he was out
of the schoolroom, the children were the victims of their own im-
pulses, to which seemed given a stronger spring by the enforced
repression. There is no order which is more than skin deep, unless
it be the free, glad obedience of the child to a law, which he per-
ceives to be creative because it enables him to do something real.
Nothing short of the union of love and thought can produce spiritual power, *i.e.*, creativeness (1906, 17–18). . . .
    We are always either educating or hindering the development of
our fellow-creatures; we are always being uplifted or being dragged
down by our fellow-creatures. Education is always mutual. The
child teaches his parents (as Goethe has said) what his parents
omitted to teach him. Every child is a new thought of God, whose
individuality is significant and interesting to others, though it is his
own limitation; and to appreciate a child's individuality is the advantage the teacher gets in exchange for the general laws which he
leads the child to appreciate. It is this variety of individuals that
makes the work of education fascinating, and takes from it all wearisome monotony. . . . Teachers who are not conscious of learning

from their pupils, may be pretty sure they teach them very little (1906, 87–88).

> Peabody stressed repeatedly the beauty of individual unique-
> ness and the important role teachers play, not only in bringing
> out the inner essence of each particular child but in teaching
> the children to appreciate and respect each other's different
> attributes.

If there are no two leaves alike, much more are there no two human individuals precisely alike, and human intercourse is made
refreshing by these various individualities playing over the surface
of the universal race-consciousness. If you respect the individuality of a child, and let it have fair play, you gain its confidence. Nothing is so delightful as to feel oneself understood. It is much more
delightful than to be admired. But to give a child's individuality fair
play in a company of children, you must open children's eyes to
one another's individualities, and you will find that if you suggest
their respecting each other's rights in the plays, there is something
within them that will justify you (1906, 168).

> Another important aspect of Peabody's kindergarten education
> was giving children the freedom to do things on their own at
> their own pace. The adult's role is to set the stage and give
> encouragement, but not to help, for that hinders the child's
> enjoyment of self-discovery and the power that comes from
> self-motivated achievement.

The child enjoys the symmetry all the more, if he feels as if he
personally produced it. This is the secret of his love of repetition.
He wants to see if by the same means he can again produce the
same effect. He does the thing again and again, till he feels that he
does it all of himself. He does not want you to help him even with
your words (and you never should help him *except* with words). If
a child acts from a suggestion, he feels free—but if he produces the
same effect, or a similar effect, without your suggestion, he has a
still more self-respecting sense of power; and his will becomes more
consciously free the more he chooses to put on the harness of order (1906, 200). . . .

The secret of power and success is *gradualism*. Any child can learn
anything, if time and opportunity is given to go step by step. Then

learning becomes as easy and agreeable as eating and drinking. Every degree of knowledge, also, must be practically used as soon as attained. It then becomes a power: makes the child a power in nature; and prepares him, when his spirit shall come into union with the God of Nature, and Father of Human Spirits, to become a power over Nature (1877, 104).

REFERENCES

Alcott, A. B. (1836 and 1837). *Conversations with children on the Gospels* (Peabody, E. P., recorder). Boston: James Munroe.

Channing, W. E. (1840). *Emancipation*. Boston: E. P. Peabody.

Froebel, F. (1896). *The education of man* (W. H. Hailman, Trans.). New York: D. Appleton.

Peabody, E. P. (1835). *Record of a school*. Boston: James Munroe.

———. (Ed.). (1849). *Aesthetic papers*. Boston: Author.

———. (Ed.). (May 1873 to December 1875 and January to December 1877). *Kindergarten Messenger*.

———. (1877). *Guide to the kindergarten and intermediate class*. New York: E. Steiger. (First published in 1864 and revised in 1869).

———. (1880). *Reminiscences of the Reverend William E. Channing*. Boston: Roberts Brothers.

———. (1906). *Lectures in the training schools for kindergartners*. Boston: D. C. Heath. (First published in 1888).

SELECTED OTHER WORKS BY
ELIZABETH PALMER PEABODY

First steps to the study of history. (1832). Boston: Hilliard & Gray.

First nursery reading book. (1849). New York: G. P. Putnam.

Last evening with Allston and other papers. (1886). Boston: D. Lothrop.

SELECTED WORKS ABOUT
ELIZABETH PALMER PEABODY

Baylor, R. M. (1965). *Elizabeth Palmer Peabody: Kindergarten pioneer*. Philadelphia: University of Pennsylvania Press.

Marshall, M. (1987). *Three sisters who showed the way*. New York: American Heritage.

Ronda, B. (1999). *Elizabeth Palmer Peabody: A reformer on her own terms*. Cambridge, MA: Harvard University Press.

Ronda, B. (Ed.). (1984). *Letters of Elizabeth Palmer Peabody, American Renaissance woman.* Middletown, CT: Wesleyan University Press.

Tharp, L. H. (1950). *The Peabody sisters of Salem.* Boston: Little, Brown.

Weber, E. (1969). *The kindergarten: Its encounter with educational thought in America.* New York: Teachers College Press.

3

Elizabeth Blackwell: Medical and Physical Education for Females

In the early 1800s, middle-class White females were supposed to know little about body functions and to abhor talk about human needs and desires. Respectable women did not become nurses, were forbidden to enroll in medical schools, and did not discuss sex even among themselves—although they were frequently pregnant and often died in childbirth or from pregnancy complications. They received little medical treatment or sympathy for their "female complaints," nor was the medical establishment much interested in gynecology or child care. In fact, what information was available was often inaccurate, of little value, and sometimes harmful.

Into this repressive arena strode a courageous woman, bent on challenging not only social mores but the formidable medical institutions that contributed to the ignorance and physical dangers of females in all social classes, and in turn to the poor health and welfare of their families. Elizabeth Blackwell was the first woman in America to receive a medical degree from a college. Barred from practicing in any hospital because of her gender, she established one exclusively for women, founded a medical school for female doctors and nurses, and spent much of her life promoting new sanitation practices in hospitals, homes, and schools.

Blackwell also severely criticized the type of teaching that passed for education in the public schools. She believed it consisted of too much book learning about subjects that were uninteresting to young minds and beyond their maturity level to understand in any meaningful way when introduced too soon. She had major concerns about the lack of physical exercise during the school day, especially for girls, and the damage to growing bodies of sitting slumped over desks for long periods. Education, she felt, was highly important for both females and males, but the curriculum and teaching methods needed to be aimed at promoting physical as well as mental growth in ways appropriate to each age level.

EARLY YEARS

Although Elizabeth Blackwell was born in England and spent the last forty years of her long life there, her major educational contributions were first made in America where her family emigrated when she was eleven years old. Born into a large, well-to-do family in 1821, she was the third child. Her early life in England was happy, healthful, and secure. Her father owned a thriving sugar refinery, which supported not only a growing family but four unmarried sisters, a governess, and several servants. He was respected as a man of integrity, but also attacked for being a Dissenter (an unpopular religious minority) and an abolitionist (although his sugar business depended on Jamaican slavery).

Samuel Blackwell was also unique in that he encouraged his daughters to read, write, and study the classics at home with his sons, who, because of their religious beliefs, were also not allowed to attend the government schools. When hard times hit England's industries following a number of riots, a cholera epidemic, and bank failures, the Blackwells sailed for America in 1832. A new sugar business was started in New York, then Cincinnati, but financial security was never again achieved. Samuel Blackwell died suddenly leaving a widow, nine children, and many debts. Stunned by this loss, Elizabeth (then seventeen) and her two older sisters opened a boarding school in their house to support the family. Later, Elizabeth taught music, French, and academic subjects in Kentucky and the Carolinas where she saw firsthand the brutality of slavery.

Returning to Ohio, Elizabeth was heavily involved in the abolitionist movement, made friends with the prominent Beecher family (she was a close friend of Harriet Beecher who later wrote *Uncle Tom's Cabin*), and became acquainted with the leaders of the Transcendentalist philosophy. For a while, the three older girls were members of the liberal Unitarian church in Cincinnati whose eloquent minister was the nephew of William Ellery Channing, the leader of Unitarianism in Boston. This early experience of independent thinking and religious and political dissension had a lasting effect on the Blackwell children, all of whom made unique, positive contributions toward a better society.

Elizabeth was not fond of teaching, however, for her female students, although pleasant, had little interest in academic studies. A few years later, a dying female friend suggested that she become a doctor. Women at the time were barred from all medical schools in America, and Elizabeth disliked anything connected with illness or the body. But, realizing the comfort a woman doctor would be to female patients, she determined to pursue this, attracted by the struggle to win a moral victory against sex discrimination. While continuing to teach, she sought out sympathetic physicians who lent her books, allowed her to attend lectures, and sent letters of recommendation to numerous medical schools, all of which rejected her application because she was female.

MEDICAL EDUCATION

Her break came in 1847 when the faculty at Geneva College in New York reluctantly agreed to accept her if the 150 male students unanimously voted her in. They did, mostly as a lark. Much to their surprise, this quiet, diminutive classmate was brilliant and studious. Medical courses at the time were not rigorous nor were many students academically serious. Elizabeth Blackwell was an exception. She proved that women were capable, won over both students and faculty, and graduated with top honors. Despite this, the college refused to accept any more female students, not even her younger sister Emily Blackwell who was equally intelligent, hardworking, and talented. Elizabeth also was not allowed to process in or sit on the stage with her male peers during their graduation ceremonies.

Blackwell's medical degree was given widespread notice, mostly favorable, although some thought her aspirations disgraceful. The *Boston Medical and Surgical Journal* said it was unwomanly to "aspire to honor and duties which, by the order of nature and the common consent of the world, devolve upon men" (Wilson, 188).

Because medical courses in America were limited and closed to women, Blackwell decided to pursue advanced studies in Paris. This was a dangerous time to be in France, for disease epidemics and revolts against Napoleon were raging. The only institution that would accept her was La Maternite, a school for midwives, where she had to live with twenty lively, poorly educated girls in one crowded dorm room. She gained excellent, down-to-earth experience, however, for most of the patients were poor unwed mothers. Many were also prostitutes. Mothers and babies were sometimes horribly disfigured by syphilis and often died of infections, many times picked up in the hospital.

It was here that Blackwell embarked on her lifelong goal of educating not only the public, but doctors themselves, about the need for cleanliness and patient comfort. Hospitals were appalling places at the time. Neither hands nor instruments were washed before surgery. Sheets and clothes were dirty and unchanged between patients. Anesthesia was only three years old and only slowly being accepted by physicians.

Blackwell intended to become a surgeon, but a tragic accident blocked those plans. While treating a baby with purulent ophthamalia, her own eyes became severely infected. She left the hospital to stay with her older sister Anna, a journalist and translator living in Paris, and for months was almost blind. Sight slowly returned to one eye, although forever impaired, but the other had to be removed and a glass one inserted. After a rest, but still determined to be a doctor, she went to London to continue medical studies with the help of well-to-do friends (including Lady Noel Byron, the poet's widow). She began writing essays and decided that prevention of disease through education about health, sanitation, and the human body would be her primary goal.

One of Blackwell's most valued friends at the time was a young English woman, Florence Nightingale, who was intent on being a nurse, against her wealthy parents' wishes. Nursing, as well as doctoring, was considered a scandalous profession for females, for no respectable woman would touch other people's bodies. "To her, chiefly," said Elizabeth, "I owed the awakening to the fact that sanitation is the supreme goal of medicine, its foundation and its crown" (Blackwell, 1895, 176). In 1851 Blackwell returned to

America, hoping some day to build her own hospital where she could institute cleanliness, train women doctors and nurses, and promote her beliefs in the importance of disease prevention.

HYGIENE, PHYSICAL, AND SEX EDUCATION FOR GIRLS

Unfortunately, little had changed in America. Despite her experience, high recommendations, and advanced studies, no hospital would accept Elizabeth Blackwell's medical degree and few patients would come to her private practice. In desperation, she advertised in a liberal newspaper a series of six lectures at two dollars each on bodily hygiene and physical education for girls, which drew a small but intelligent audience. Particularly receptive to her ideas and work were female members of the Quaker community.

This was Blackwell's first public-speaking effort, but she was effective. Speaking simply and firmly, she presented information that was clear and practical. At a time when the words "sex" and "body" were offensive and taboo, her talks were sensational and courageous. Later published under the title, *The Laws of Life, in Reference to the Physical Education of Girls* (1852), the lectures dealt with sanitation and hygiene, the process of sex and birth, and the structure and function of both female and male bodies. Blackwell urged girls to stop wearing tight clothing and encouraged them to run, jump, climb, and dance, stressing the Greek ideal of unity of mind and body. She was criticized for challenging sexual mores, but her progressive views won a following and gave an impetus to her stalled career.

MEDICAL CONTRIBUTIONS

With the help of friends, mostly Quakers, Dr. Elizabeth Blackwell opened a free clinic in one of the worst slums of New York City. In the neighborhood, poverty-stricken immigrants knew no English, families of twelve lived in one or two filthy, unlit rooms and pigs from a nearby slaughterhouse ran loose. The stench was intolerable and cholera epidemics were frequent. The death rate for both babies and mothers during childbirth was exorbitant.

The prevailing means of treating problem pregnancies included bleeding, leeches, opium, stomach purging, and bed rest. In contrast, Blackwell advocated exercise, nutrition, sunlight, soap and water, protection of food from flies, fresh air, less clothing, and no drugs—or doctors, except herself. Many nights she walked alone to deliver babies in areas dangerous even in daylight. Insults were hurled at her in the streets and threatening letters were common. "Woman doctor" was associated in the public mind with deadly, back street abortions, a connection women physicians were long overcoming.

With her sister, Dr. Emily Blackwell, who fought a battle against discrimination to graduate with honors from the Medical College of Cleveland, Ohio, and Dr. Marie Zakrzewska, a German immigrant who earned a medical degree from the same college, Dr. Elizabeth Blackwell opened the New York Infirmary for Indigent Women and Children in 1857. Staffed entirely by women, it received the endorsement of several prominent and courageous male physicians who served on the board despite hostility from the medical establishment. Elizabeth became the director and Emily, who was better skilled medically, the chief physician and surgeon.

The infirmary was funded by an annual bazaar, plus lectures, concerts, private donations, and a yearly grant of one thousand dollars from the state. Later, a training school for nurses was established, the first in America. During the Civil War, the school was a major supplier of nurses for clinics and hospitals treating wounded soldiers. In 1865, more than thirty-one thousand patients were served, including many Black refugees from the South, with 640 hospitalizations. Only five patients died—a record far below normal and especially impressive considering the clientele's poor living conditions. Four years before Lister's work on antiseptic principles, the doctors at this women's hospital washed their hands in a carbolic solution before attending patients—a practice scorned by many physicians at the time.

In 1868, after raising thirty thousand dollars, the Blackwell sisters opened the Woman's Medical College of the New York Infirmary. Although other women's medical schools now existed, the Blackwells considered them inadequate. Unless female students underwent a course of study equal to that offered males, they believed, women would never be as qualified to practice medicine or be accepted by hospitals and the public. They insisted, therefore, that this school have the most advanced curriculum available, thorough examinations, and a substantial endowment to ensure a continued existence. They instituted innovations unavailable at even the men's medical colleges: an optional three-year course (considered unnecessary), strict hygiene supervision, a chair of hygiene (held by Elizabeth), emphasis on disease prevention, and a board of examiners separate from the teaching staff. The board included some of the most respected male physicians in New York, giving needed prestige to the new college. There were seventeen women students in the first class, including several who later became prominent in their own right.

Another of Elizabeth Blackwell's unique contributions was the appointment in 1866 of a "sanitary visitor," who invited herself into slum area homes to teach the importance of ventilation, cleanliness, nutrition, and economics. The first appointee was Dr. Rebecca Cole, the first African-American woman in history to earn a medical degree. The Blackwells' hospital and medical school, thus, was not only uniquely staffed by female physicians, but the first to hire racial minorities and to teach the poor about health and nutrition in their own homes.

CRITICS

Although she exemplifed many of the highest ideals of intelligent, independent womanhood, Elizabeth Blackwell has often been taken to task for her "antifeminist" remarks. She was a fearless fighter for the causes she believed in, broke the barrier that excluded women from the medical profession, and helped other females enter the science field. Her goal, however, was freedom of opportunity rather than legal rights. Unlike some leaders of the women's movement in her day, she did not spurn marriage and domestic life—in fact, she believed that most women should be wives and mothers—but realized that combining this with a demanding career was an impossibility at the time.

Blackwell chose a nontraditional path for herself and helped others who wished to do so. However, she knew the pain and sacrifice this entailed and did not disdain those who lived more typical lives, nor did she urge most women to follow her example. On the contrary, she used her education, skills, and leadership abilities to further the welfare of all women and their families by improving health, knowledge, and living habits. Although not opposed to the women's suffrage movement in principle, she elected to devote her time and efforts to furthering educational opportunities and other societal goals.

Blackwell's quarrel with some of the feminist leaders (but not with her sisters-in-law Lucy Stone and Antoinette Brown Blackwell) was over what she perceived to be an "anti-man" stance. She had adored her father, remained close to her brothers, and was frequently dependent on the financial and professional support of male relatives, friends, and doctors. Although rejected by the medical establishment, she did not blame men in general. "I have had too much kindness, aid, and just recognition from men to make such attitude of women otherwise than painful; and I think the true end of freedom may be gained better in another way . . . I must keep my energy for what seems to me a deeper movement" (Blackwell, 1895, 178–179). She felt that gaining the vote would change little related to improving the daily lives of women and children. Furthermore, despite progressive ideas about equality, many feminist leaders were still influenced by their Puritan upbringing, aghast at Blackwell's public lectures on sex and body functions, and felt it improper for women to enter the medical field. In these ways she was far more advanced than they.

Blackwell was frequently criticized by male physicians, not only for helping women become doctors and nurses, but for pushing such "unnecessary" practices as washing hands, equipment and sheets, using anesthesia, treating patients with sympathy and respect, and for expanding the medical curriculum.

In England, she was attacked for urging the poor to stop having large families, for castigating industries' unsafe working conditions and phosphorous poisoning, and for arguing for health insurance, old-age pensions, and better housing. An animal lover, especially of dogs, she also angered medical researchers for her protests against vivisections.

LATER YEARS AND LASTING ACHIEVEMENTS

When Elizabeth was nearing fifty, a rift developed between the Blackwell sisters. The hospital and school were thriving under the excellent medical and organizational skills of Emily, who inwardly resented her older sister's control and authoritarian manner. Recognizing this, and always the restless pioneer, Elizabeth decided to leave the institutions in the capable hands of her sister and devote her energies to broader educational pursuits. At the urging of English friends, she went back to her home country to do for women there what she had done in America.

For the next forty years, Dr. Elizabeth Blackwell lectured on hygiene and sanitation, helped women enter science professions, fought prostitution, and promoted the discoveries of Lister and Pasteur. She formed the national Health Society in England and with Dr. Elizabeth Garrett Anderson and Dr. Sophia Jex-Blake, both of whom had been encouraged and inspired by Blackwell's earlier work, she helped establish the London School of Medicine for Women and held the Chair of Gynecology.

Like most women leaders of the time, Elizabeth Blackwell had to make a choice between career and family, but not without an emotional struggle. In Paris there had been mutual attraction between herself and the young French doctor who taught obstetrics and treated her eye, but knowing that matrimony would end her medical aims, she rejected the possibility. Although she never married, she had a long-time companion and confidante. To fill maternal yearnings and assuage her loneliness, she took in a seven-year-old orphan named Katharine Barry. Never legally adopted, Kitty became an accepted member of the Blackwell clan and a close friend of Elizabeth's niece, Alice Stone Blackwell. She spent the rest of her life devoted to the woman she called "My Doctor" or "Aunt Bessie."

Until disabled by a fall in her last years, Elizabeth Blackwell continued to publish books and articles on numerous subjects, including the autobiographical sketches called *Pioneer Work in Opening the Medical Profession to Women* (1895). After a long courageous life, filled with disappointments and hard-fought battles as well as many achievements, Blackwell died in 1910 at age eighty-nine. She was buried in Kilmun, Scotland, a favorite vacation spot. Later, her beloved Kitty Barry was placed beside her.

In 1958, Hobart and William Smith College (formerly Geneva College), Geneva, New York, instituted an annual Elizabeth Blackwell Award for "outstanding service to mankind." The purpose was to yearly honor a woman whose life exemplified Blackwell's "unselfish devotion, sense of dedication, and reverence for life." The college's decision in 1847 to accept this nontraditional student has had long-lasting benefits, not only to women but to the world.

Excerpts from Elizabeth Blackwell

Early in her medical career, Dr. Elizabeth Blackwell gave a series of six well-received lectures to mothers and their teenaged daughters. Called *The Laws of Life, in Reference to the Physical Education of Girls* (1852), she discussed how to raise healthy, happy daughters. She was criticized by others, however, for her audacity in addressing matters pertaining to the female body. In contrast to societal norms, she urged mothers to dress their daughters in loose-fitting clothes, encourage them to play and exercise, and give them nutritious meals.

Think of this, oh mothers! when you see your young daughters growing up around you, remember that it is in your power to render them healthy and strong in body, and the mothers, in their turn, of a stronger race than ours, or to subject them to the disease and suffering which enfeebles the present generation. Do not continue in the fatal error of our age—forcing the intellect, and neglecting the development of the body—do not sacrifice to the false beauties of fashion the higher beauty of health, of happiness, and of usefulness (33). . . .

We have seen that in order to provide for the gradual development of the body, we are bound to furnish the conditions favorable to its organic growth, by leaving each function in entire freedom to perform its work, and by furnishing those materials that are necessary to this work. Moreover, as the child grows, the necessity arises for uniting mental with bodily training; we must provide for the growth *of the mind through the* body, by making the exercises of the physical nature, the expressions of ideas and emotions.

Now we shall find, on reflecting upon the method in which we educate our children; in examining the details of their daily life . . . that the whole *scope of education* is diametrically opposed to the true principles of growth, and that with every advancing year of the child's life, there is an increasing violation of Nature's law (122).

Blackwell lambasted public schools and the harm they did to children's bodies, spirit, and true intellectual growth. She pushed for homes and schools to be changed into safe, healthy, worthwhile places for all children. Schools, she insisted, did physical damage to the developing bodies of both sexes as they sat hunched over desks, books, and lengthy writing assignments.

Let us consider first our system of school education, which embraces the most important period of youthful life. The large majority of children enter school about the age of 7 years—they leave at the age of 16. Now this period embraces, you will remember, all those remarkable changes of bodily organization which occur, from the establishment of second dentition, to the attainment of puberty—a period of rapid growth—when the body is enlarging its range of action for the powers already established, and acquiring new functions of immense importance to the individual and to the race, and when consequently the body makes incessant demands upon the vital energy, and requires the most favorable circumstances to perform its work well (122). . . .

Now what do we do, at this period of special physical growth? We completely ignore the body; we substitute mental for physical training; we entirely change the order of nature, and oppose the most formidable obstacles to the *proper* growth of the body.

For, to ensure this proper growth, the appropriate nourishment of every physical function must be supplied in abundance. Thus a constant supply of fresh air is essential, and large amounts of *exercise* in the open air, with plenty of simple nourishing food; the body never grows so well, as in the companionship of the trees and flowers and streams of a healthy country district.

The great object of the child's life is school—pure intellectual training. The best part of every day, generally from 9 to 3, is spent in the school-room, where the mind is forced to long and *unnatural* exercise; and in order to meet the tasks imposed upon it, it must either rouse itself to a constant exertion, that would be difficult for an adult, or it must rest contented with half understanding its studies, and learn by rote; a habit which is injurious to the best qualities of the mind. And this unnatural exercise is carried on under circumstances which would almost seem expressly calculated to injure the body as much as possible. The imperfect ventilation of our houses, which renders it extremely difficult to preserve a purity of atmosphere, even in a private family, makes it quite impossible to keep the atmosphere of our school-rooms fit for human lungs to inhale; it is difficult in summer-time, with all the windows open, to maintain an entirely pure air where so many human bodies are congregated for hours together; but during the greater part of the year, the windows must be shut—for several months the rooms must be artificially heated, generally with stoves, and often red-hot.

Under these circumstances, the essential constituents of the air are exhausted more rapidly than they can be supplied; the atmosphere is laden with human exhalations, and becomes a slow poison to those who breathe it—the lungs continue to take it in, but it can no longer perform its office of fully purifying the blood—the blood is unable to supply the normal stimulus to the brain, and the child is forced to make more difficult efforts to perform its studies well. . . .

A playground is very seldom connected with the school; once or twice during the six or seven hours of school-time, the child may go down for five minutes into the yard—there may be half an hour's intermission in the middle of the day—but there is no provision for amusement; the children are exhausted by the morning's efforts, they lounge about and eat their luncheon, and are not, for the most part, inclined to take bodily exercise.

There is another serious evil, besides the close air of the school-room; it is the injurious position in which a great part of the time is passed, leaning over the desks in study or writing. This position is exceedingly mischievous: the chest, which should expand freely to receive the air, to strengthen its muscles and grow, is cramped and contracted by this stooping attitude, and the pressure against the desk; the shoulders, which should be thrown back at an equal level, are thus drawn forwards, and the right one thrown upward by the action of the arm in writing, often retains this position, and we have the narrow chest and crooked shoulders so commonly seen in school-girls. The seats are hard, generally without backs; the body is wearied by a constrained position, exhausted by mental efforts; the muscles of the back cannot maintain with vigor the upright position; they seek to relieve themselves of the weight of the head and back by awkward attitudes—leaning on one side, resting on the desk, curving the back. This effort continued day after day weakens the muscles, often distorts the spine, and produces other bodily deformities—for it must ever be borne in mind, that they are the *young*, not adults that we are educating—growing bodies, soft and pliable, that give way to undue pressure, and cannot resist evil influences with the power of older years (123–126).

> Female intellectual faculties were neglected by society, Blackwell believed, but in contrast to other educators who urged that a rigorous academic curriculum be instituted for adolescent girls, she considered these subjects too abstruse, un-interesting, and impractical for young minds of both sexes.

Studying books and subjects too early to be understood kills
children's eagerness to learn, she maintained, and blocks them
from the valuable insights they would gain later from topics
encountered at a more appropriate level of maturity.

The instruction given at school, is almost purely intellectual; the
senses receive little regular training; their power is used in very
moderate degree to aid the mind—yet they are the first teachers
of the young. Grammar, history, definition, composition, call for
simple intellectual exertion—the natural sciences are very slenderly
illustrated by sensible examples, and the poor engravings in the
textbooks are often the only illustration they receive. The most ab-
struse subjects, that tax the attention of the strongest mental powers,
are presented as studies for the young: girls of 13 or 15 are called
upon to ponder the problems of *mental and moral philosophy*, to demonstrate the *propositions of Euclid*, to understand the refinements of
rhetoric and logic—admirable studies, truly, but they are the food of
mature minds, not suitable to children (127). . . .

It would puzzle the most ingenious observer, to discover the *good
use* of most of our children's studies. If the object be mental discipline, there is no surer way of defeating such an object, than to attempt to give the mind a superficial view of a subject too difficult
for it to grasp—to confuse it with a multitude of disconnected
studies—to hurry it from subject to subject, so that the simple studies more suited to the young mind, are imperfectly acquired, and
soon forgotten. Thus the greater part of the time devoted to the so-
called cultivation of the intellect is really wasted; and it is no uncommon thing, to find the young girl who has gone through all the
English branches, quite unable to write a lady-like note, or read
aloud a single page with right emphasis, ease and accuracy.

How can it be otherwise, when the young mind has to apply it-
self, during the limited term of school-study, to such a list of sub-
jects as the following: Grammar, Ancient and Modern History,
Natural Philosophy, Chemistry, Botany, Astronomy, Mental and
Moral Philosophy, Physiology, Rhetoric, Composition, Elocution,
Logic, Algebra, Geometry, Belles-Lettres! (128). . . .

These studies will be completely dropped and soon forgotten—
for they were *learned too soon*—the mind could not retain them—
they were acquired too superficially, too unpractically, to be of any
use in strengthening the understanding, or aiding in daily life. . . .
Little *real knowledge* is gained, but an evil habit of mind has been

acquired; a habit of careless, superficial thought, an inability to apply the mind closely to any subject. . . . What a result is this, for years of time spent and much money—surely we may call it a criminal waste of life! (137). . . .

The teacher is not to blame for this wretched system of cramming. He is compelled to present as formidable an array of knowledge to be acquired at his school, as his neighbors do; and most patiently and earnestly he may strive to aid his pupils in the acquisition. The evil is in the system itself, which substitutes names for things; which fails to recognize the necessity of adapting the kind of instruction to the quality of the mind. . . . This system is radically wrong—no effort of the teacher can make it right (128–129).

> The limited freedom given to girls and their lack of physical activity, particularly when compared to their brothers and male classmates, was of special concern to Blackwell.

The school-hour closes, the [female] child returns home; not racing merrily along, with shout and frolic—the little girl must not slide on the ice with boys—she must walk properly through the streets; she dines, and then there are lessons to be prepared for the next day; if she be a docile, obedient child, some hours will be spent in this preparation—if the instincts of nature are too strong, she will neglect the lessons, wander about the house, perhaps join in a game of play; and the next day she will suffer the penalty of a reproof from the teacher, for imperfect lessons, and the loss of her place in the class.

Perhaps the child is sent out to take a walk, on her return from school; but what is there attractive or invigorating in a walk through our streets? Can there be a more melancholy spectacle than a boarding-school of girls, taking their afternoon walk? there is no vigor in their step, no pleasure in their eye; the fresh air is certainly good for their lungs, but the unattractive exercise is of most questionable benefit (129–130). . . .

Thus under the combined influences of confinement and close air, of unsuitable food, and injudicious mental excitement, the school-days pass; under such influences the child changes from a girl into a woman; such is the foundation laid for the important duties of adult life!

If we were to sit down and carefully plan a system of education, which should injure the body, produce a premature and imperfect development of its powers, weaken the mind, and prepare the individual for future *uselessness*, we could hardly by an ingenuity construct a system more admirably calculated to produce these terrible results . . . by their very conformity to rules, by striving to please their teachers and parents, and maintain an honorable position—they fall completely into the snare, and sin against nature, in exact proportion to their obedience to society! (133–134).

> Elizabeth Blackwell's criticism of schooling, especially for girls, was harsh and no doubt justified. In her own family, the females had been given considerable freedom. They were encouraged to study what they found interesting, to be practical and independent thinkers, and to be physically active. Thus, she proposed a plan for improving schools that she believed would much better prepare girls for productive and satisfying lives as women.

We must cease to force the learning of a later period upon the youthful mind. . . . A system of scientific gymnastic training should be adopted—every kind of active sport encouraged—the accomplishments of riding, dancing, singing, swimming, archery, etc., should be taught. . . . The *habits* of the intellect should be carefully trained in conversation and in those studies which are suitable to the age; these studies should be such as require the aid of the senses—writing, drawing, the study of charts and maps, the living languages and a variety of other subjects, might be employed to advantage. There should be frequent expeditions into the country or to the sea-side, where in direct intercourse with nature, the child in conversation with its teacher, would learn with the utmost avidity and happiness (178). . . .

There is a Divine Order of Growth appointed for the human being, which we dare not neglect without violating our duty as parents . . . which, if we observe faithfully through every period of life, will bring health and beauty, and happiness amongst us. We shall see our children grow up around us in strength and grace, and fulfill in after life the promise of their childhood (180).

REFERENCES

Blackwell, E. (1852). *The laws of life, in reference to the physical education of girls*. New York: Putnam.

———. (1895). *Pioneer work in opening the medical profession to women*. With
　　Dr. Emily Blackwell. London: Longmans.
Wilson, D. C. (1970). *Lone woman: The story of Elizabeth Blackwell*. Boston:
　　Little, Brown.

SELECTED OTHER WORKS BY
ELIZABETH BLACKWELL

Address on the medical education of women. (1864). With Dr. Emily Blackwell.
　　New York: Baptist & Taylor.
*Counsel to parents on the moral education of their childen in relation to sex, under
　　medical and social aspects*. (1879). New York: Brentano; London:
　　George Bell, 1913.
Wrong and right methods of dealing with social evil. (1883). London: D.
　　Williams.
Essays in medical sociology. (1892, 1899). London: Ernest Bell. 2 volumes.
The human element in sex. (1894). London: Churchill.

SELECTED OTHER WORKS ABOUT
ELIZABETH BLACKWELL

Baker, R. (1944). *The first woman doctor*. New York: Messner.
Chambers, P. (1956). *A doctor alone*. London: Bodley Head.
Hays, E. R. (1967). *Those extraordinary Blackwells*. New York: Harcourt,
　　Brace & World.
McFerran, A. (1966). *Elizabeth Blackwell: First woman doctor*. New York:
　　Gross & Dunlap.
Whittier, I. (1961). *Dr. Elizabeth Blackwell: The first woman doctor*. Brunswick,
　　ME: Brunswick.

4

Ellen Swallow Richards: Science Education for School, Home and Society

Although few people recognize her name today, in the late 1800s Ellen Swallow Richards was a nationally known woman. An outspoken activist in science, higher education for females, and the application of scientific principles in the home and society, she was highly respected by leaders and the general public. She also was a thorn in the flesh to industrial owners, school officials, and the conservative male-dominated science establishment. Her accomplishment as the first woman to graduate from and to teach at the Massachusetts Institute of Technology (MIT) and the first woman in America to earn a chemistry degree was followed by many other "firsts" and high achievements.

Ellen Richards opened doors for women in higher education and science careers, educated the public about nutrition and environmental dangers, initiated the ecology movement, founded the Home Economics Association, and dedicated her life to improving the welfare of all society. She wrote fourteen books and numerous articles, gave hundreds of speeches across the nation, and traveled worldwide as a consultant on chemical, environmental, and education matters.

EARLY YEARS

Born Ellen Henrietta Swallow in 1842 in a small town in Massachusetts, she was an only child of schoolteachers turned farmers, then shopkeepers. She learned early to manage the house alone because her mother, like many women at the time, was often ill—a situation that influenced Ellen's later work as an applied scientist. There were no labor-saving devices to lighten housework. Water for washing clothes, dishes, and bodies had to be carried from wells. Cooking kettles were heavy. Mattresses, made of straw, had to be aired and carpets beaten. Bread was baked daily and garments, bedding, and draperies sewed by hand.

Additionally, water was polluted by human and industrial wastes, knowledge of sanitation was meager, airtight homes poisoned lungs, food was poorly preserved, diseases had no cures or preventatives, and doctors believed illness was hereditary and a natural state for females. The ideal woman was supposed to be delicate and frail, but in reality most did physically difficult work in environments that undermined their health. Frequent pregnancies and the demands of motherhood further sapped their strength. That many women became feeble is not surprising.

Education was another problem because schooling for girls was still considered by the general public to be a waste of time. Ellen was home-schooled until age sixteen, briefly attended an academy for girls, then returned home to work in the store and care for the house and her sickly mother.

In 1865, at the end of the Civil War, the first female college, Vassar, opened in Poughkeepsie, New York, offering the same curriculum as men's institutions. For three years, Ellen worked to earn money for tuition and studied to pass the entrance exams. She entered Vassar at age twenty-six, excelled especially in chemistry and astronomy, and graduated in two years. Later, despite the fact that chemistry was not a field open to women and MIT did not admit females, Ellen applied to that college to do advanced studies. Reluctantly, the faculty voted to admit her—at no charge—so they could officially say that no woman was enrolled. Thus, at age twenty-eight, Ellen Swallow was the first woman to attend classes at MIT.

She was such a brilliant student, however, that a prominent MIT professor chose her to help with the Massachusetts water sanitation project—the first in the nation. The professor sailed for Europe to observe work there and left Ellen alone to do the meticulous analysis and record-keeping, in addition to her regular studies.

At age thirty, Ellen Swallow received a bachelor of science in chemistry from MIT, becoming the first degreed woman chemist in America. She did private consultations, then married an MIT engineering professor, Robert Richards. Although marriage at the time usually ended a woman's career, her husband supported Ellen's work and, having no children, they were both able to lead rigorous professional lives. They also frequently entertained students and Boston intellectuals in their attractive home, which had the latest and most efficient scientific inventions.

CHEMISTRY ACHIEVEMENTS

Besides her lifelong involvement in education, Ellen Richards did significant work as a chemist. Analyzing a copper ore sample, she discovered nickel, which began a valuable industry in Canada. Her discovery of cottonseed hull composition and a way to remove grease from wool brought her worldwide recognition. Press coverage of her attacks on adulterated and dishonestly labeled food and drugs eventually led to the Pure Food and Drug Act of 1907. She also made the first analysis of spontaneous combustion of commercial oils, which became the basis for establishing fire insurance rates.

In 1884, MIT established a Laboratory of Sanitary Chemistry with Ellen Richards as assistant director, making her the first female instructor at an all-male college. Although she is seldom given credit, it was her idea to use chlorine content as a guide to ascertain sewage content in water, a major advance in sanitation that has saved countless lives. She also produced the first water quality standards in the United States. Richards received many honors in her lifetime for her valuable scientific contributions, including being the first woman elected to both the American Association for the Advancement of Science and the American Institute of Mining Engineers.

Only one major disappointment scarred her productive life. After serving ten years as a chemistry instructor at MIT, she applied to study for a doctorate. The board and faculty, however, felt it unsuitable to award MIT's first PhD in chemistry to a woman and rejected her application. Despite this discrimination, she remained on the staff the rest of her life, in addition to conducting valuable work outside the university for the betterment of society.

SCIENCE EDUCATION AND TEACHER TRAINING

In the 1870s, both education and science were expanding rapidly in America. Secondary schools for boys and girls were growing in number and course offerings. The instructors, many of them now female, were expected to teach the new sciences, which they often knew little about. When teachers at the Girls High School in Boston begged for help, Richards persuaded MIT to let her have an unused garage for a women's science laboratory. However, she was given no equipment or salary for this extra work. Raising the funds herself for apparatus, she taught the course for several years until the college, noting its success, opened a well-equipped laboratory with a paid male instructor. Primarily benefiting MIT male students, women teachers were also admitted, but the person who began the enterprise was once again snubbed.

Because females were still barred from getting advanced science degrees, Richards founded an association to help them do research at the Zoological Station on the Gulf of Naples. In 1881, she also helped establish what became the outstanding Marine Biological Laboratory at Woods Hole, Massachusetts, and set up an annual one thousand dollar science competition for female researchers. In these ways, she hoped to break the male dominance of science, to open opportunities for women, and to convince more females to study science, teach science, and choose science-related careers.

TEACHING METHODS

"We teach too much," said Ellen Richards. "The child is far quicker than the adult to grasp what is suited to him. We present to him something he cannot grasp—the large end—and he wisely refuses it. We call him stubborn when he is only wise. We forget that the abstract is arrived at only after much experience with the concrete" (Clarke, 1973, 202–203). What children require, she maintained, is less teaching and more opportunity to simply experiment on their own.

Richards heartily endorsed the work done with mentally and physically disabled children by her friend Samuel Gridley Howe, especially his principle of giving students more control. She encouraged her college students to take individual initiative, but believed that even the very young benefit from having more say over their learning. "Place the child in an environment rich in suggestion," she urged. "Furnish the [natural] materials for discovery. [The child] needs pleasant surroundings—color, form, flowers, music—to express his ideas and to stimulate imaginative thoughts . . . to become master of his environment" (Clarke, 203–204).

In the late 1800s, Richards argued that schools badly needed reforming, with less rote learning, more hands-on experimental activity, and a broadening of the curriculum beyond basic skills. She criticized instructors for failing to apply knowledge, especially science, to everyday life: "The true value of science teaching, the knowing for certainty, the investigation for one's self, in contrast to mere belief or blind acceptance of statements, is missed in much popular teaching" (Hunt, 181). The aim of education, she wrote, is "to give young people that power of acquiring knowledge all their lives and not to stuff into their heads [in a few years] enough to last a lifetime!" (Clarke, 107). Richards believed that students need to be actively doing, linking all their senses to the mind:

> What we do to kill learning! We put young children on hard seats, in cramped positions, force into their heads a dead book which must not be crumpled or torn, and exclaim: "Study! Study! Recite!" And this when human instinct demands objects to be handled and put together. . . . It is contrary to all the laws of [human] development to allow the child to pull to pieces [in learning] without putting together. (Clarke, 203–204)

Early in her teaching career, Richards had a revelation that influenced her educational philosophy. She was giving classes on minerals to both young children and schoolteachers at Boston's Museum of Natural History and was surprised to find the children grasping things much more quickly than the adults. As an experiment, she taught the same class to some Harvard undergraduates, who were also slower to learn and more dependent on the instructor and books. She surmised that the children trusted their own observations and were thus able to identify and classify minerals easily and competently. Older students and adults had learned to doubt themselves and therefore looked to others to guide and evaluate their judgments. Schools, she concluded, must teach students to observe for themselves, use this evidence in making decisions, and apply what they learn to their own lives. In this way they become independent thinkers, capable of resisting unwise advice or manipulative actions of others. This philosophy guided her teaching methods the rest of her life, with all ages of students.

Richards pushed for science to be started in early elementary grades in order to teach observation, reasoning, and judgment, but insisted that this learning be done with natural objects, not out of books. Teachers, she stressed, should take children outdoors, or bring in flowers, minerals, shells, dried insects, and fibers, rather than coop the students up in closed rooms memorizing isolated facts.

With ideas that sound very contemporary, Richards recommended that public schools become "community centers," using evenings and weekends for adult and family education. Since the schools, because of critical social problems, had become in essence "foster homes," they might as well be used to advantage to counteract the negative forces that were destroying family life, community cohesion, and individual esteem and hope. Like the progressive educator John Dewey, Richards maintained that schools should teach ideals and values in addition to skills and knowledge and "should not teach how to make a living before they teach how to live" (Clarke, 204).

EDUCATION OUTREACH

Ellen Richards' contributions, like those of other educators discussed in this book, went far beyond the typical classroom. Education was more than formalized schooling; it encompassed the whole of human lives and included all age groups and levels of ability. Although she believed schools to be very important, she demonstrated that teaching can and should take place wherever there is a need and people are ready to learn. Using the lecture platform, media, professional journals, home study lessons, museums, women's clubs, and private laboratories, as well as college and public school classrooms, Richards continually promoted science education and involved students of all ages in experiments, applications, and self-study.

Environmental Education

According to biographer Robert Clarke, in 1892 Ellen Richards launched the *oekology* movement, as she called it, at a banquet speech for a prestigious club in Boston (1973, 114). Concerned about the deteriorating environment from industrialization and the poor health of citizens, especially women and children, she explained her goal of using science and education to improve the quality of air, water, food and sanitation in homes, schools, and society. At the time, however, the cause of illness, as well as poverty and ignorance, was believed by leading scientists to be hereditary. Furthermore, "applied" science was scorned by those working in the "pure" sciences. Richards's work to improve health and welfare by upgrading the environment was rejected or ignored, and the ecology movement faltered with her death in 1911 until revived in the mid-twentieth century.

Despite resistance, Richards wrote a number of books about the critical need to stop pollution and improve environmental conditions (see a partial list at the end of this chapter). The thrust of her work was in a 1910 book called *Euthenics: The Science of Controllable Environment, A Plea for Better Living Conditions as a First Step Toward Higher Human Development*. An earlier book, *The Art of Right Living* (1904) had a section on teaching children about environmental concerns.

Science Education for Adults

Another of Richards's interests was improving home conditions through science education. Women, she felt, needed information in three areas:

1. How to safeguard their family's health.
2. How to do home chores while saving labor.
3. How to obtain the most quality for their money.

Although she herself was a nontraditional career woman, she worked hard to improve the lives of those whose primary work was the care of home and children. In the women's laboratory she created at MIT, Richards focused on chemistry that was important to homemakers: why bread crust turns brown, what soaps and cleaning fluids are made of, how to know if something has been adulterated. She wrote two textbooks that were widely used in classrooms: *The Chemistry of Cooking and Cleaning* (1882) and *Food Materials and Their Adulterations* (1886).

In her own home, Richards practiced what she taught: sanitation, economy, efficiency, and health. She used light-weight rugs in place of heavy carpets, and short, washable curtains instead of draperies. She rejected the dust-catching Victorian decor in favor of rooms that were spare, light, and uncluttered. Laden with career responsibilities, she bought a newly invented vacuum cleaner and gas stove and hired live-in maids (often students) to help clean house, cook meals, and entertain guests. This way cleanliness and health could be maintained, while leaving time for work and pleasure.

Home Study in Science

Another education project for adults, to which Richards devoted many hours for twenty years with negligible pay, was the science section of Boston's Society to Encourage Study at Home. Correspondence courses were offered to women who lived in isolated areas across America. Richards designed lessons in geology, mineralogy, geography, and botany and wrote letters and comments to each student by hand (typewriters were not yet invented). Thousands of women wrote her about domestic concerns. She drew up house plans and menus, advised about sanitation and clothing, and answered all questions with practical suggestions. Most importantly, she urged women to balance physical work with mental stimulation, to put housework in proper perspective, to find enjoyment, and to take good care of themselves as well as their families.

Advanced Education for Females

Because girls were forbidden to enroll in the prominent Boys' Latin School in Boston, Richards and her friend Julia Ward Howe (author of "The Battle Hymn of the Republic") helped open the Boston Girls' Latin School in 1878 so that young females could receive the same academic education as their male peers and be better prepared to enter the newly established women's colleges.

In 1881, Richards helped establish the organization that significantly advanced the cause of higher education for women: the Association of Collegiate Alumnae, later changed to the American Association for University Women (AAUW). When that group refused to allow southern women graduates to join, Richards founded a Southern Association of College Women with the same goals of raising money for scholarships and encouraging bright females to attend college. She also served for years on the Executive Council of the National Education Association (NEA).

Nutrition Education

Ellen Richards's first venture in educating about nutrition was aimed at low-income families. In 1889, with the aid of a partner, she opened a public kitchen in Boston where the wage-earning poor, who worked ten or more hours in factories, could buy cheap, nourishing, ready-cooked food and take it home. This was a revolutionary idea. Canned goods were few and poor in quality and carry-out food unheard of. Named the "New England Kitchen," the menu included vegetable and pea soup, cornmeal mush, beef stew, fish chowder, and Indian and rice pudding. Customers were encouraged to view the clean kitchen, the cooking process, and the sanitation practices. Other such kitchens were also opened, but unfortunately the appeal was more to the middle class than to the poor, and after three years all were closed. The experiment, although failing to achieve its original goal, did lead to a focus on nutrition in settlement houses, to improved meals in prisons, orphanages, and hospitals, and to lectures for medical students on proper food for patients.

To continue educating the public about nutrition, Richards designed an exhibit for the Columbian Exposition in Chicago in 1893 that included a model kitchen and small restaurant selling healthful lunches. Food charts decorated the walls, attractive leaflets were sold, and cards listing the meals' nutritional values given out. More than ten thousand people were served in two months. While in Chicago, she also introduced nutrition ideas to the staff at Hull-House, the settlement established by Jane Addams to meet the needs of the immigrant poor on the squalid Southside.

Because of this success, the Boston School Committee asked Richards to provide lunches for students to replace the junk food sold by janitors and neighboring stores. Her New England Kitchen took over the operation, an enormous undertaking that had to be privately financed, and thus began the nation's first public school hot lunch program. At age fifty-five, Ellen Richards was the foremost authority in America on the preparation of low-cost, high-nutrition meals. Her advice was sought by asylums, orphanages, prisons, and hospitals and a series of bulletins was produced for the U.S. Department of Agriculture.

CRITICS

In addition to the criticisms engendered by attacking industrialists for polluting the environment; government officials for ignoring the dangers to food, air, and water; male scientists for devaluing applied science and excluding women; and physicians for their lack of knowledge about diseases and disinterest in disease prevention, Richards took on the educational establishment for its unconcern for children's health and safety. In an 1896 speech at the American Health Association convention, she claimed that two hundred children were "murdered" each year through environmental neglect in public schools. One-half of Boston's school buildings, she said, were dangerous places where open sewer pipes, filthy toilets, unclean floors, no ventilation, and few fire escapes killed many students each year by preventable diseases and school fires. Boston teachers had the highest death rate in the nation. School houses are "unwashed," she said, and "danger lurks in the drinking cups and among the towels" (Clarke, 161).

This exposé of school conditions created powerful enemies among administrators, but the public outcry forced Massachusetts to legislate school safety measures, and soon other states followed. Additionally, when Richards took over the first school lunch program in the nation, she alienated the janitors and neighboring store owners who had been making money by selling food to students. Some of the parents were also upset, believing their children were being used as guinea pigs for one of Richards's scientific experiments.

HOME ECONOMICS

Most of these achievements were accomplished before Richards, at age fifty-seven, embarked on the venture for which she is most known in education—establishing the American Home Economics Association and serving as its first president. In 1899, she met with nine other women at the Lake Placid, New York home of Melvil Dewey (of Dewey Decimal fame) to plan for the inclusion of home economics courses across the land, from grade school to colleges.

The purpose was to use a scientific basis for all aspects of domesticity, such as nutrition, sanitation, budgeting, and time management, and to make this into a distinct and respectable discipline.

Richards saw the emphasis on the improvement of homes and family life as an extension of her prior work in science education, environmental issues, the application of chemistry to everyday life, and the advancement of women in professional careers. Home economics required research, knowledgeable and competent teachers, the latest in scientific equipment, and well-produced curricular materials. Much of the initial planning and writing was done by Richards herself. As a part of her work in dietetics, for instance, she introduced radical changes in cooking by quantifying measurements and standardizing the ingredients, an approach later carried out by Fannie Farmer in her popular cookbooks.

Home economics, as Richards envisioned it, was a major reform in U.S. education for its purpose was to apply scientific principles in the home. Because women did most of the daily planning, spending, and caring for basic needs, they should have a sound education in nutrition, consumer economics, hygiene, and health. The goal was to elevate homemaking to its rightful place as a crucial element in the well-being of the family as well as an interesting and creative endeavor requiring intelligent choices based on accurate and up-to-date information.

LATER YEARS AND LASTING ACCOMPLISHMENTS

In 1878, Richards was admitted to the American Association for the Advancement of Science, an honor normally given only to those who have done valuable research beyond the doctorate. Although denied the opportunity to earn a PhD at MIT because of her gender, she finally received an honorary one from Smith College, Northampton, Massachusetts, in 1910. A small bronze plaque was eventually placed on the wall of MIT's chemistry building in honor of her many achievements and a lifetime of teaching at the college.

The name of Ellen Swallow Richards is unknown to most people today, but her astounding accomplishments have lived on to the betterment of all of society. Her battles for pure food, air, water, and soil and her pronouncements against unsafe school buildings not only brought these dangers to the public's attention but resulted in legislation that greatly improved the health and welfare of children and adults alike.

As an educator, her influence was far-reaching, touching on every age group, and included many aspects in and beyond the classroom. She encouraged active learning, practical application of knowledge, and student initiative and control. She fought for sanitation, nutrition, and safety in public schools, pushed for science education at all levels and better training for teachers, created opportunities for women to gain higher education and engage in scientific careers, and established home economics nationally as an important part of the public school curriculum.

Ellen Swallow Richards died of heart failure in 1911 at age sixty-eight, shortly after giving another public address about the importance of applied sciences. At her request, she was cremated and her ashes placed in a cemetery in Gardiner, Maine. The year that Richards died, the great French chemist Madame Marie Curie, after receiving her second Nobel Prize, came to the United States and gave only one formal presentation, which she called "Ellen Richards Monograph."

Excerpts from Ellen Swallow Richards

Richards had a long list of achievements in science and education before turning her attention to what she is most known for today, the movement to teach home economics in public schools. In an 1897 article entitled "Domestic Science: What It Is and How to Study It at Home," she advocated the teaching of domestic skills as an applied science and criticized those who disparaged such studies by saying they lacked rigor and content.

Domestic Science may be defined as the application of all modern scientific knowledge to the administration of the home. It is eminently an *applied* science, and, because it is practical and comprehensive, educators in general have looked very much askance at it, and have put aside those who have advocated its adoption as one of the topics in the school curriculum, with the assertion that it was too crude and too indefinite to be given a place as a mentally nutritive subject. It is, however, not by keeping an acorn on a shelf, but by planting and watering it, that a strong tree is produced.

Since this topic was first suggested, both bacteriology and sociology have sprung up and have become accepted university studies, and "oecology" is still held at arm's length. There is, evidently, at the bottom of this reluctance a fear of the changes which would inevitably result from a serious study of the problems of Home Life. One reason for this is not far to seek. Women are conservative, and time and much convincing proof are needed to induce them to change their habits of life. A great respect for tradition and authority leads them to doubt the wisdom of new ideas (1897, 1078). . . .

If the house itself demands study on broad lines, the provision of suitable food for the family requires even more, and that not only in detail but on general principles. Chemistry, physics, physiology, and a dozen other sciences have contributed to the present knowledge on the subject. The mother, who provides the food through the assimilation of which the child derives the energy that enables it to comprehend its lessons or accomplish any task, has not the least important office in the education of the child. When the function of food is better understood by the housewife, the science of nutrition will be studied with more zeal. . . . If women once become convinced of the value of this knowledge, they will find ways of acquiring it (1897, 1080).

> Home management rightly done, believed Richards, required the skills of professional positions held by males, including engineering. In her book *Euthenics* (1910), she claimed that if women used the latest knowledge in applied sciences, they could transform the care of home and children into a challenging and interesting, as well as practical, endeavor that would greatly improve the family's health and welfare through good nutrition, clean air, sanitation, and fiscal prudence.

The work of homemaking in this engineering age must be worked out on engineering principles, and with the cooperation of both trained men and trained women (152–153). . . . The Home Economics Movement is an endeavor to hold the home and the welfare of children from slipping over the cliff by a knowledge which will bring courage to combat the destructive tendencies (156). . . .

Household engineering is the great need for material welfare, and social engineering for moral and ethical well-being. What else does this persistent forcing of scientific training to the front mean? If the State is to have good citizens, productive human beings, it must provide for the teaching of the essentials to those who are to become the parents of the next generation. No state can thrive while its citizens waste their resources of health, bodily energy, time and brain power, any more than a nation may prosper that wastes its natural resources.

The teaching of domestic economy in the elementary school and home economics in the higher is intended to give the people a sense of *control* over their *environment* and to avert a panic as to the future.

The economics of consumption, including as it does the ethics of spending, must have a place in our higher education, preceded in earlier grades by manual dexterity and scientific information, which will lead to true economy in the use of time, energy, and money in the home life of the land (1910, 158–159).

> Cleanliness in all aspects of living was of utmost importance to Richards, but especially in schools. In an article called "The Need of Sanitary Schools" (1903), she gave specific engineering instructions for how this should be accomplished and railed against those who refused to spend the money necessary to build schools that protected the health of the students.

About thirty years ago we defined sanitation as clean soil, clean air, and pure water. Today we may add three more requirements: good food, cheerful surroundings, and freedom from noise. . . .

A sanitary school building, once the site is right, demands at least three things: Plumbing in a separate stack, or, if in the cellar, then a separate ventilating shaft which is always working. Quick removal of used air as well as of used water. This cannot be done unless the construction permits. When windows are depended upon, they must reach the ceiling and not stop three feet below, leaving an inverted lake of hot, bad air to fluctuate back and forth, but not to be removed until it cools, which often does not take place during the day. . . . The inlets [of the ventilation system] must be so placed as not to cause a draught upon the teacher's head or the scholars' bodies, for swiftly moving air has the chilling effect of cold air . . . I believe the ideal plan would be to have the warmed air come up through the floor through many inlets and rise steadily to the ceiling, pouring out into a flue with a sufficiently strong upward draught to keep the current moving at such a rate as to give fresh air for each inhalation of the child when sitting, and diluted air when standing and for the teacher. . . .

Our schoolhouses are built to be an ornament to the city, perhaps; but they are frequently copies (to save architects' fees) of some other city's blunder, or the contractor bungles the fairly good plans. In almost every case it is the children who are sacrificed, who are dragged by the truant officer from the sunlight and free air of the streets into stagnant, dusty, ill-smelling air which no respectable Board of Charity would allow in an almshouse; and yet the strong arm of the law confines our children by the thousands in buildings without fire escapes, in buildings where the walls and floors are covered with dust containing scarlet fever and diphtheria germs.

Let us have a twentieth-century school house in which it will be possible to educate a twentieth-century child—in which a well-trained, refined man or woman will be willing to teach. . . . Let us cut loose from tradition and have a school house in which the whole child may thrive—not only his mind, but his body. Not only give him clean air and washing facilities, but cheerful, uplifting surroundings and good food . . . I believe the day is not far off when the town schools with two sessions will provide a noon lunch instead of sending the small children through wet, muddy streets to a home from which the mother may be absent, to pick up as they may such food as they find. Even if the food is right, may it not be possible to utilize the noon hour to better advantage in teaching gardening, housekeeping, or in games? (807–808).

> The school was taking over the roles previously played by the home, not by choice but by necessity, claimed Richards. In *Euthenics* (1910), she maintained that parents were neglecting their duties and expecting teachers to instruct in the classroom what should have been taught long before in the home. The school, she said, should not displace the home, but rather teach knowledge and skills that equip children to lead better lives.

The school is fast taking the place of the home, not because it wishes to do so, but because the home does not fulfill its function, and so far has not been made to, and the lack must be supplied (78).

The home is responsible for the upbringing of healthy, intelligent children. Here is the place for fostering the valuable and suppressing the harmful traits. The school can never take the place of the home in this. With the large classes of the public schools, the teacher should not be asked to undertake this individual work. . . . The office of the home must be to teach habits of right living and daily action, and a joy and pride in life as well as responsibility for life. It is not fair that the parents should sit back and shift to the school the whole responsibility for the future citizen (81–82).

[The home and the school]: One must not displace the other, for one cannot replace the other, but rather the home and the school must react on each other. The home is the place in which to gain the experience, and the school the place in which to acquire the knowledge that shall illuminate and crystallize the experience. The child should go out to the school with enthusiasm, and return to the home filled with a deeper interest and desire to realize things (91).

Not only has the home put the burden of education on the school, but the school has drawn the child away from the home. The school of today demands much more from him than the school of the early New England days. It has taken the time that was formerly given to assisting in the duties of the household; it has taken from the home the interest and responsibility that were developed through the cooperation in the family life. School has taken the place of home in the child's thoughts. In the morning the thought is of reaching school in time, not of the home duties whose performance could lighten many a mother's burden. . . .

The interest awakened in the school will surely react upon the home. It is like an expedition going out to make discoveries and to bring back knowledge to its own land. The directive work of the school will thus become a practical realization in the home. Then the cycle will be complete, for while the school has separated the child from his natural environment for many hours and weeks, it is sending him back better equipped through knowledge and experience to fulfill his place there (94–95).

> Richards had much faith in the power of public schools, if well-supported and well-conducted, to improve the lives of whole families and the future generations. In her book, *The Art of Right Living* (1904), she stressed the need for schools to teach attitudes as well as knowledge so that students would become well-rounded individuals who took pleasure in both life and work. The public school, she believed, "is the natural medium for the spread of better ideals" (36) and the authorities who make school-related decisions are very short-sighted when they fail to see that well-constructed buildings, up-to-date knowledge, and the teaching of right living not only enhance the well being of children but of the whole community.

Education is not complete unless all powers work together. Brain gymnastics are no more commendable than bodily gymnastics as mere exercises, and if one-sided are as fatal to all-around development (7–8). . . . We hear much of the need of educating the child for life, but little or nothing of teaching him *to live* so that life may be worth living (37). . . .

[The] joy of self-control should be taught to children. Control of *things* comes easily then; control of *self* comes with greater difficulty, but patiently taught does become habit (20). . . .

An important adjunct in the art of right living [is] joy in work. . . . We cannot too strongly impress upon the child how important to health is work . . . not necessarily remunerative in the coin of the realm, but in satisfaction with one's life. Work is necessary in order to enjoy recreation (27). . . .

[The] inner sense of ineffectiveness is the unrecognized cause of the restless discontent so prevalent today. No person who is accomplishing something, seeing it grow under his hands to what it was in his thought, is discontented. . . . The true pleasure of work is in the doing and not in the possession afterwards, in most cases (29). . . .

In life our keenest pleasures are not those we seek so earnestly, but side lights upon our pathway, unexpected happenings. If one lives for pleasure, one does not enjoy life in the degree possible to one who lives for work and finds his pleasure unexpectedly (31). . . . Give a child an end for which to work, and he will willingly bend his energies to the task (38).

It is a curious superstition, this conservatism of the school men in regard to what it is permissible to teach . . . they go so far to neglect the resources developed before their very eyes for the promotion of health and efficiency.

If all our schoolhouses were built and cared for as well as the present state of scientific knowledge permits, the efficiency of the children now using them would be raised two hundred per cent in ten years' time. In our zeal for the mind, we have starved and dwarfed the body (43). . . .

Since the future depends upon the children it behooves us to see to it they have a fair chance (47). . . . Knowledge [should] be given to the pupil as fast as substantiated by scientific investigation. Thereby lives are saved, the state is enriched, general happiness is promoted (50).

REFERENCES

Clarke, R. (1973). *Ellen Swallow, the woman who founded ecology.* Chicago: Follett.

Hunt, C. (1912). *The life of Ellen H. Richards.* Boston: Whitcomb & Barrows.

Richards, E. S. (1882). *The chemistry of cooking and cleaning: A manual for housekeepers.* Boston: Estes & Lauriat.

———. (1886). *Food materials and their adulterations.* Boston: Estes & Lauriat.

———. (1897, April 24). Domestic science: What it is and how to study it at home. *The Outlook,* 1078–1080.

———. (1903, August 1). The need of sanitary schools. *The Outlook,* 807–808.

———. (1904). *The art of right living.* Boston: Whitcomb & Barrows.

———. (1910). *Euthenics: The science of controllable environment, a plea for better living conditions as a first step toward higher human development.* Boston: Whitcomb & Barrows.

SELECTED OTHER WORKS BY ELLEN SWALLOW RICHARDS

First lessons in minerals. (1882). Boston: Rockwell & Churchill.

Guides for science teaching. (1886). Boston: D. C. Heath.

Domestic economy in public education. (1899). *Educational Monographs.* New York: New York Teacher's College

Sanitation in daily life. (1907). Boston: Whitcomb & Barrows.

SELECTED OTHER WORKS ABOUT ELLEN SWALLOW RICHARDS

Bryant, A. G. (1936). *Mrs. Ellen H. Richards and her place in the world of science.* Poughkeepsie, NY: Vassar College Archives.

Douty, E. M. (1961). *America's first woman chemist: Ellen Richards.* New York: Messner.

Lam, T. K. (1981). *Science and culture: Ellen Swallow Richards and 19th century nutritional science.* Baltimore, MD: Johns Hopkins University.

Yost, E. (1943). *American women of science.* Philadelphia: Frederick A. Stokes.

5

Jane Addams:
Educating the Immigrant Poor

A wave of immigration brought many thousands of poor to Chicago's Westside around the turn of the nineteenth century. Men, women, and children alike were forced to work in factories for long hours in unhealthy, unsafe surroundings. They were frequently ill, given pitiful wages, lived in unsafe tenements, had poor nutrition, and received little if any medical care. Those too young to work were often left alone at home, sometimes tied to a bed or chair, or in warm weather were locked out to wander the streets until parents or older siblings returned.

Appalled by this sea of misery, a young, wealthy woman committed her life to fighting for better living and working conditions, civil rights, compulsory education, and child labor laws. Perhaps even more important, she brought enlightenment and dignity to those of all ages whose minds and lives were being stultified by lack of opportunity to learn, discuss, share skills, and create.

In her older years, Jane Addams was probably the most admired woman in America, but hardships, heartache, and criticisms had frequented much of her life. Tuberculosis of the spine in infancy left her with a crooked gait, tilted head, and a lifelong feeling of homeliness, although she was an attractive woman with an engaging personality. She had several unsuccessful operations in an attempt to correct her spinal problem and was in frequent ill health.

Undergirding Addams's political and social endeavors was an educational theory that bridged the chasm between institutions and everyday life for the thousands of working poor in the slums of Chicago. Hull-House, the settlement house she established, was more than a charity institution. It was, for Addams, a continual research project on how to actualize the social ethics of democracy and meet the needs—educational, economic, social, and personal—of poverty-stricken immigrants in America.

EARLY YEARS

Dedication to the poor was not the expected life for a child born into a wealthy family. Jane Addams's father, the owner of a prosperous flour mill in Cedarville, Illinois, was a state senator for sixteen years, a personal friend of Abraham Lincoln, and the town's most respected citizen. His wife died in childbirth in 1862 after her ninth pregnancy, when Jane was only two years old. Mr. Addams, who later remarried, cherished this frail child with the crooked back and nurtured her intelligence and passion for learning. When he died suddenly a few weeks after Jane's graduation from Rockford Seminary in Illinois, she became severely depressed. Against her stepmother's wishes, she enrolled in the Women's Medical College in Philadelphia intending to be a doctor. Going to college was unusual enough, but for a woman of breeding to study medicine was then considered outrageous.

Addams's medical career, however, was short-lived. Besides not liking the studies, she underwent a spinal operation that left her bedridden for six months. Additionally, doctors told her she could never bear a child, which was a traumatic revelation that brought back the depression. Accompanied by her stepmother and friends, she took the antidote typical of wealthy young women in her day—a two-year grand tour of Europe.

What impressed her most, however, was not the art and architecture, which she loved, but the squalid poverty in the cities. Addams came back to America haunted by the misery she had seen. For three more years she floundered, unwilling to lead a life of cultured ease, but not knowing what else to do. On a second trip to Europe, she visited settlement houses in London and this time returned with a clear vision.

At age twenty-nine, with her college friend Ellen Gates Starr, Addams went to Chicago in search of a building to launch her mission. They found it on Halstead Street. A once elegant suburban mansion, Hull-House now sat in the worst slums of this large city, dilapidated but restorable. The women could not afford to buy the house, named for its original owner, so in 1889 they rented rooms on several floors, cleaned and painted to bring back the earlier beauty. Soon neighbors were flocking to the door to seek help. According to Addams's account in *Twenty Years at Hull-House,* first published in 1910, by the end of the first year, fifty-thousand people had come to Hull-House for one reason or another, and by the end of the second, two thousand were being served a week.

EDUCATION AT HULL-HOUSE

The purpose of Hull-House and all settlements, said Addams, was to be an "experimental effort to aid in the solution of the social and industrial problems which are engendered by the modern conditions of life in a great city. . . . It is an attempt to relieve, at the same time, the overaccumulation at one end of society and the destitution at the other" (1910, 125–126). A central feature of this experimental effort was education, not just of children but of people of all ages, and the use of talents wherever they were found. Besides the Hull-House residents, who were all women of high intelligence, ability, and moral commitment,[1] men and women from many walks of life and areas of Chicago volunteered to help the indigent improve their intellectual as well as physical lives.

Eventually, the immigrants themselves were recruited to teach skills they learned in the Old World that were not used or valued in the industrial slums. Settlement founders showed that in all social classes were people with specialized knowledge that would enrich human culture. "We make foreign birth a handicap to them," wrote Addams, "or we may make it a very interesting and stimulating factor in their development and ours" (1930, 409–410).

Most of all, the settlements taught democracy as a way of life, not as an abstract theory devoid of concrete application. Democracy, believed Addams, is a system of ethics grounded in action, which demands as its base a belief in the worth and equality of all human beings, no matter what their race, religion, ethnic background, age, or gender. "As democracy modifies our conception of life," she said, "it constantly raises the value and function of each member of the community, however humble he may be" (1964, 178). The penalty of a democracy is that "we are bound to move forward or retrograde together. None of us can stand aside; our feet are mired in the same soil, and our lungs breathe the same air" (1964, 256).

There was no religious instruction at Hull-House, but an encouragement for people of all faiths to work, study, and play together harmoniously. Although Addams was born of Quaker parents, she attended no church and subscribed to no particular dogma, except a strong belief that the greatest good lies in helping humanity. Clubs were organized that offered the opportunity for discussion, debate, and dissent. To Addams, however, action was "the sole medium of expression for ethics . . . a situation does not really become moral until we are confronted with the question of what shall be done in a concrete case, and are obliged to act upon our theory" (1964, 273).

Meeting Life's Needs

In 1889, according to Addams, over one million people lived in Chicago and nearly three-fourths were foreign born or first-generation Americans. In Ward 19, where Hull-House stood, nineteen different nationalities were represented by the inhabitants. Most lived in pathetic situations, in small wooden houses or overcrowded tenements. Streets were filthy, plumbing was inadequate, garbage was uncollected, basements were wet and smelly, fire escapes were nonexistent even in factories and schools. There were 255 saloons in the ward, but only seven churches. Sweatshops abounded, with much of the work done by women and children. No legislation existed to protect their rights or safety.

One of the first projects established at the settlement was a day nursery for preschool children who were being locked up in tenement rooms or left to wander the streets while their parents worked long hours. For a few cents a day, the children received good supervision and a nourishing meal. A kindergarten soon followed, and later the first playground in Chicago was built on the site of several demolished houses. Clubs for older children were held in the afternoons and evenings for those in school or working in factories. A boys' club had classes in wood, metalwork, photography, electricity, and printing to help the boys discover their talents and train for jobs—all taught by volunteer workmen. For girls and women, in the tradition of the day, classes were held in cooking, sewing, millinery, and other domestic and occupational crafts.

In the evening, adults came to Hull-House for education, help with legal or other problems, and socializing. From the beginning, college extension courses were offered in literature, philosophy, and political science. Enrollments were always full. Groups with such names as the Shakespeare Club, the Arnold Toynbee Club, the Chicago Question Club, and the Lincoln Club were popular. The settlement's large hall could seat 750 people, and Sunday evening lectures were jammed. The Hull-House theater, which presented plays by Shakespeare and Moliere for adults and "Snow White and the Seven Dwarfs" for children, also drew enthusiastic crowds.

As soon as money could be found, the programs and the buildings were expanded. The gymnasium offered organized sports and a public bathhouse. More than forty different activities—from Sunday concerts to boarding houses for single males and females—brought education, culture, and hope to the immigrant masses in Chicago's teeming Westside.

Interestingly, the first building to be added to the original mansion was an art gallery, furnished with works that Addams had brought back from her two trips to Europe and from family possessions. The arts, she believed, were the universal means of communication. She wrote, "To feed the mind of the worker, to lift it above the monotony of his task, and to connect it with the larger world, outside of his immediate surroundings, has always been the object of art" (1910, 435). Later, a public kitchen was opened where cheap nutritious meals were available. To the surprise of Hull-House residents, however, the art gallery remained the more popular, confirming Addams's belief that art is as basic a need as food in human lives.

A Hull-House innovation that is taken for granted today was unique in the 1800s. Addams became distressed that immigrant children were often ashamed of their parents' values, customs, and talents, which created a cleavage between the generations. This was augmented by the need of parents to depend on their children, who learned English at school, to act as interpreters of both the language and customs of America. To impress on both the immigrant youth and native-born Americans the value of Old World skills, classes were set up in Hull-House in spinning, weaving, embroidery, and other crafts that no longer served a useful function in a big city, but that demonstrated the artistic talents of the older generation. Soon, the young people of the area developed a respect for their parents' and grandparents' skills and enrolled in classes taught by people who before had felt useless and demeaned. A Labor Museum was set up to display their crafts, and lectures on the history of industrial labor were given in order to "recover for the household arts something of their early sanctity and meaning" (1910, 242).

Learning from Everyday Life

Addams believed that public schools in her day had limited capabilities for advancing democracy and equalizing opportunities. By putting emphasis on reading and writing, educators seemed to assume that "the ordinary experience of life is worth little, and that all knowledge and interest must be brought to the children through the medium of books" (1964, 181). Elected to Chicago's Board of Education in 1905, Addams often angered both teachers and administrators by her criticism of curriculum and methods. She believed, along with her friend John Dewey,[2] that schooling should not be an isolating experience, divorced from life. Public schools, she said, bring children inside, away from the streets and home environment, and give them no tools for dealing with the poverty and industrial society in which they live.

Education at Hull-House, on the other hand, was intimately connected with life outside its walls. Addams believed that education is not a transmission of knowledge, but an interaction between pupil and instructor, who teach each other how to use knowledge to improve their lives. Anything was considered educational that helped and united people, and learning was viewed as a lifelong venture. Thus, besides the day nurseries and kindergartens, clubs were established for children and adults of all ages, in whatever seemed of interest. Concerned that schools gave children little opportunity to develop initiative, imagination, and social relations, Hull-House clubs encouraged these skills, as well as gave supplementary instruction in school subjects for those who needed it. Addams was especially worried about those who left school at age fourteen to take dull, tiresome jobs in factories, so she organized social clubs and evening classes to enrich and enliven their lives.

Many evening university extension courses were offered for adults, but finding professors able to relate to the clientele was difficult. Teaching in a settlement house required "tact and training, love of learning," and the conviction that it will help people "whose intellectual faculties are untrained and disused" (1965, 33–34).

Those instructors who were successful had to rid themselves of all rigidity and constraints and offer a simple delight in knowledge.

People who work long hours with meaningless details, wrote Addams, do not want specialized information but courses in the "wonders of science" or the "story of evolution" (1964, 215). They want "to hear about great things simply told" (1965, 197). Addams was convinced that the best education of the time was being done in settlement houses, not in public schools or even expensive, private universities, for only in places like Hull-House were the powers of individuals being liberated and connected to the rest of their lives. She joined the Chicago Board of Education in hopes of improving education in public schools by redesigning the curriculum to make it more appealing to students and incorporating the kinds of holistic and humanistic methods that were so effective in the work with immigrants, from early childhood to aging adults.

INTEGRATION OF EDUCATION
AND OTHER REFORMS

In addition to her efforts in organizing the settlement activities, Addams was actively involved in local and national politics for the betterment of women and children in particular, and the poor in general. At this time, with her public esteem high and her influence considerable, she was able to pressure the Illinois legislature into passing the first factory law, which improved sanitary conditions and regulated age fourteen as the youngest a child could be employed. She continued her efforts for labor rights and in 1904 was elected vice president of the National Women's Trade Union League. However, an eight-hour work day law for women, which they lobbied for and the state legislature passed, was ruled unconstitutional by the Illinois Supreme Court.

Addams angered graft-taking politicians by fighting for regular garbage collection and better sewers in her neighborhood. The mayor, one of the few political leaders sympathetic to her causes, appointed Addams the garbage inspector of her ward. She arose early to inspect the men at their work, sued landlords for not providing proper garbage collection, and insisted on increasing the number of refuse wagons. She also worked for laws prohibiting the sale of narcotics and impure milk, for research on the causes of the typhoid epidemic, for regulations on the qualifications of midwives, for support for deserted wives and children, for insurance for widows, and for damages for workers injured on the job. Clearly, she lived her belief that education encompassed all of life, rather than something done only to children, only in schools, and only from books.

LATER YEARS

In 1909, Addams was the first woman elected president of the National Conference of Social Work. In the same year, she helped found the National Association for the Advancement of Colored People (NAACP) and served on its national board until her death. She was also on the national committee of the American Civil Liberties Union (ACLU), founded in 1920, for its first ten years. In 1910, she became vice president of the National Women's Suffrage Association. Because of her work with the poor, Addams was appointed during World War I to head the Department of Food Administration to oversee the distribution of scarce food supplies. She then turned her energy toward world peace. Influenced by her pacifist Quaker background, she saw war as directly related to the oppression of women. The glorification of war and its use as a means of settling international disputes, she argued, is not only inhumane but contributes to keeping women in an inferior status, because females have less physical strength and did not at the time in most countries serve as soldiers.

Before America's entrance into World War I, which she vigorously opposed, Addams organized the American Women's Peace Party, which by 1916 had forty-thousand members. She also helped establish the Women's International League for Peace and Freedom and served as its president for fourteen years. When she received the Nobel Prize for Peace in 1931, she donated the sixteen-thousand-dollar prize money to the League.

CRITICS

Jane Addams was denounced by such groups as the American Legion and the Daughters of the American Revolution (DAR) for her opposition to World War I and her efforts in promoting peace. She was viewed by many as a traitor to the nation and the admiration for her unselfish humanitarianism dissolved into hatred for her "un-American" activities. Her most unpopular cause was the fight for justice on behalf of immigrant anarchists and revolutionaries, most of them Russians. She was called "a factor in a movement to destroy civilization and Christianity" (Downs, 173). Her reputation suffered greatly until the 1930s economic depression and the New Deal efforts to help the poor. The Nobel Peace Prize, awarded in 1931 because of the very activities that earlier brought harsh condemnations, restored her to the status of national heroine in the public eye.

Addams was also vilified throughout her life by political enemies for her social reform campaigns. She and the other Hull-House residents were continually engaged in causes that invoked the wrath of businessmen and political bosses, who considered the settlement to be a nest of dangerous radicals. Infuriated by her drive to enact child labor laws, both industrial managers and poor parents who depended on their youngsters' meager income, tried unsuccessfully through intimidation and bribes to stop this movement.

LASTING ACHIEVEMENTS

Four years after receiving the Nobel Peace Prize, Jane Addams died of cancer at age 75, the same year she received the American Education award. Her dream of erasing the causes and results of poverty in her Chicago neighborhood were never realized, however, for Hull-House was still surrounded by slum dwellings, whose inhabitants worked long hours in dismal jobs for very low wages. Nevertheless, her tireless efforts had helped in many ways. By 1935, most states had enacted child labor laws and industrial safety regulations. Many communities had established sanitary codes, public playgrounds, and adult education programs. In 1920, the Nineteenth Amendment securing women's suffrage, which Addams had worked for, was finally passed.

In her long and full life, the once quiet, shy, genteel Addams was an outspoken, persuasive proponent of many unpopular but moral causes. She wrote articles and books, gave innumerable speeches to national and international audiences, received fifteen honorary university degrees, and worked steadfastly, whether reviled or revered, on matters of education, civil rights, economics, and peace.

What Jane Addams is most remembered for is the settlement house she established at the beginning of her career, giving lifelong education to the oppressed, offering programs to meet the needs of individuals and groups, and using as teachers anyone with a useful skill to create a community and build pride and self-respect. The aim of Hull-House was to "bring into the circle of knowledge and fuller life, men and women who might otherwise be left outside" (1930, 404). A settlement, she said, "is above all a place for enthusiasms, a spot to which those who have a passion for the equalization of human joys and opportunities are early attracted" (1910, 184). Although Hull-House did not ease the poverty, its education and social programs brought enthusiasm, knowledge, opportunities, and pleasure into the lives of thousands of disadvantaged immigrants of all ages.

Excerpts from Jane Addams

In her first autobiography, *Twenty Years at Hull-House* (1910), Addams told of the early years of the settlement house. After purchasing and renovating the once elegant mansion that now stood in the middle of one of the poorest, most dilapidated areas of Chicago, Jane Addams and her friend Ellen Starr set about to inform the area residents that the women were there to help in whatever ways were needed. Curious but cautious, the neighbors slowly began to investigate and test the newcomers' good intentions, until by the end of second year, more than two-thousand people were served in some capacity per week. Within the first few weeks, a major need became obvious—a nursery for the small children locked in or locked out of their tenements during the day while parents and older siblings worked, many of whom roamed the streets unsupervised, poorly clothed, and often unfed.

We early learned to know the children of hard driven mothers who went out to work all day, sometimes leaving the little things in the casual care of a neighbor, but often locking them into their tenement rooms. The first three crippled children we encountered in the neighborhood had all been injured while their mothers were at work: one had fallen out of a third-story window, another had been burned, and the third had a curved spine due to the fact that for three years he had been tied all day long to the leg of the kitchen table, only released at noon by his older brother who hastily ran in from a neighboring factory to share his lunch with him. When the hot weather came the restless children could not brook the confinement of the stuffy rooms, and, as it was not considered safe to leave the doors open because of sneak thieves, many of the children were locked out. During our first summer an increasing number of these poor little mites would wander into the cool hallway of Hull-House. We kept them there and fed them at noon, in return for which we were sometimes offered a hot penny which had been held in a tight little fist "ever since mother left this morning, to buy something to eat with" . . . Hull-House was thus committed to a day nursery which we sustained for sixteen years (167–169).

> Addams and the other Hull-House residents fought for child labor laws that would limit the hours minors could work and the type of work for which they could be employed, plus the establishment of safety rules and adequate pay. Eventually, they pushed for compulsory schooling so that children could not be hired to labor long hours at bone-wearying jobs during their years of mental and physical development. These laws were opposed not only by legislators and factory and mine owners, but by poor parents who depended on the meager income their children could bring home.

Our very first Christmas at Hull-House, when we as yet knew nothing of child labor, a number of little girls refused the candy which was offered them as part of the Christmas good cheer, saying simply that they "worked in a candy factory and could not bear the sight of it." We discovered that for six weeks they had worked from seven in the morning until nine at night, and they were exhausted as well as satiated. The sharp consciousness of stern economic conditions was thus thrust upon us in the midst of the season of good will. . . .

The visits we made in the neighborhood constantly discovered women sewing upon sweatshop work, and often they were assisted by incredibly small children. I remember a little girl of four who pulled out basting threads hour after hour, sitting on a stool at the feet of her Bohemian mother, a little bunch of human misery (198–99).

> Addams became troubled by the rift that often occurred between immigrant children and their parents or grandparents. The young people, who more easily learned English and more quickly assimilated into American life, began to view their elders with some disdain. The youth rebelled against patriarchal

authority, were embarrassed by Old Country ways, and neither understood their older relatives' difficulty in adjusting to a new culture nor appreciated their skills and talents. Addams was determined to rectify this situation.

An overmastering desire to reveal the humbler immigrant parents to their own children lay at the base of what has come to be called the Hull-House Labor Museum. This was first suggested to my mind one early spring day when I saw an old Italian woman, her distaff against her homesick face, patiently spinning a thread by the simple stick spindle so reminiscent of all southern Europe. I was walking down Polk Street, perturbed in spirit, because it seemed so difficult to come into genuine relations with the Italian women and because they themselves so often lost their hold upon their Americanized children. It seemed to me that Hull-House ought to be able to devise some educational enterprise, which should build a bridge between European and American experiences in such wise as to give them both more meaning and a sense of relation. . . . Suddenly I looked up and saw the old woman with her distaff, sitting in the sun on the steps of a tenement house. . . . The occupation of the old woman gave me the clue that was needed. Could we not interest the young people working in the neighboring factories, in these older forms of industry, so that, through their own parents and grandparents, they would find a dramatic representation of the inherited resources of their daily occupation. If these young people could actually see that the complicated machinery of the factory had been evolved from simple tools, they might at least make a beginning towards that education which Dr. [John] Dewey defines as "a continuing reconstruction of experience." They might also lay a foundation for reverence of the past which Goethe declares to be the basis of all sound progress (235–237).

> After finding women and men in the neighborhood who were skilled at a variety of primitive methods of spinning, the teachers at Hull-House mounted an exhibit showing these in historic sequence and connecting them with the then-present method of factory spinning. They did the same with weaving and other such arts. Additionally, Saturday night demonstrations of these early forms of labor were held, so that visitors could admire the skills involved, children would learn to appreciate the talents of their elders, older immigrants could take pride in

displaying their craftsmanship, and both the commonalities among the many cultures and their uniquenesses would become evident.

Within one room a Syrian woman, a Greek, an Italian, a Russian, and an Irishwoman enabled even the most casual observer to see that there is no break in orderly evolution if we look at history from the industrial standpoint; that industry develops similarly and peacefully year by year among the workers of each nation, heedless of differences in language, religion, and political experiences (237). . . . Far beyond its direct educational value, we prize [the Labor Museum] because it so often puts the immigrants into the position of teachers, and we imagine that it affords them a pleasant change from the tutelage in which all Americans, including their own children, are so apt to hold them (240–241).

> The Hull-House residents also established social clubs for the many young people living in their neighborhood, which provided opportunities for engagement in dramatic productions, debates, book discussions, dances, and other social and communal events.

I am constantly cheered by greetings from the rising young lawyer, the scholarly rabbi, the successful teacher, the prosperous young matron buying clothes for her blooming children. "Don't you remember me? I used to belong to a Hull-House club." I once asked one of these young people, a man who held a good position on a Chicago daily, what special thing Hull-House had meant to him, and he promptly replied, "It was the first house I had ever been in where books and magazines just lay around as if there were plenty of them in the world. Don't you remember how much I used to read at that little round table at the back of the library? To have people regard reading as a reasonable occupation changed the whole aspect of life to me and I began to have confidence in what I could do" (345–346).

> An important part of Hull-House education involved the arts. The first building that was erected contained a lighted art gallery, filled with paintings that Addams and others had brought from Europe, "some of the best pictures Chicago afforded" (371). This remained the finest gallery in the city until the

> Chicago Art Museum was established, and was especially ap-
> preciated by the older immigrants for whom paintings were a
> source of solace and a nostalgic reminder of their cultural heri-
> tage. Included also were art and music lessons, Sunday after-
> noon recitals, concerts, and lectures that were well attended by
> people from other parts of Chicago as well as the neighbor-
> hood, and dramatic presentations of works by such writers as
> Sophocles, Shaw, Ibsen, and Galsworthy.

The latter [three playwrights] are surprisingly popular, perhaps
because of their sincere attempt to expose the shams and pretenses
of contemporary life and to penetrate into some of its perplexing
social and domestic situations. Through such plays the stage may
become a pioneer teacher of social righteousness.

I have come to believe, however, that the stage may do more than
teach, that much of our current moral instruction will not endure
the test of being cast into a lifelike mold, and when presented in
dramatic form will reveal itself as platitudinous and effete. That
which may have sounded like righteous teaching when it was re-
mote and wordy, will be challenged afresh when it is obliged to
simulate life itself (391).

> Classes were also held in the domestic arts, such as photogra-
> phy and printing, and also working with wood, iron, brass,
> copper, and tin—taught by men and women experienced in the
> trades who helped young people of low socioeconomic status
> discover their interests and aptitudes and gain some work
> skills. Additionally, the Hull-House gymnasium was very
> popular and athletic contests brought not only enjoyment but
> relief from the tediousness of daily labors.

The Settlement strives for that type of gymnastics which is at
least partly a matter of character, for that training which presupposes abstinence and the curbing of impulse, as well as for those
athletic contests in which the mind of the contestant must be vigi-
lant to keep the body closely to the rules of the game. . . .

Young people who work long hours at sedentary occupations,
factories and offices, need perhaps more than anything else the freedom and ease to be acquired from a symmetrical muscular development and are quick to respond to that fellowship which athletics
apparently afford more easily than anything else (442–443).

Addams was convinced that education and cultural opportunities were not only the right of all people in a democracy but were essential for each soul's happiness. Moreover, the finest aspects of culture were understood and enjoyed by those from all socioeconomic levels if presented in interesting, accessible ways. The best proof of this could be found in the activities offered by settlement houses such as Hull-House.

The Settlement casts aside none of those things which cultivated men have come to consider reasonable and goodly, but it insists that those belong as well to that great body of people who, because of toilsome and underpaid labor, are unable to procure them for themselves. Added to this is a profound conviction that the common stock of intellectual enjoyment should not be difficult of access because of the economic position of him who would approach it, that those "best results of civilization" upon which depend the finer and freer aspects of living must be incorporated into our common life and have free mobility through all elements of society if we would have our democracy endure (452).

NOTES

1. Among the many who at one time resided and worked at Hull-House were Emily Greene Balch, Nobel Peace Prize winner in 1964; Alice Hamilton, physician and professor of medicine; Edith Abbott, first Superintendent of the Immigrants Protective League, and her sister Grace Abbott who succeeded her; Julia Lathrop, head of the U.S. Children's Bureau; and lawyer Florence Kelly, chief executive of the national Consumers League.

2. The great U.S. philosopher and educator John Dewey delivered lectures at Hull-House on social psychology and was a member of the first Board of Trustees. One Hull-House resident was a teacher in Dewey's laboratory school at the University of Chicago, run by his wife. Teachers in both places frequently exchanged ideas.

REFERENCES

Addams, J. (1910). *Twenty years at Hull-House*. New York: Macmillan.
———. (1930). *Second twenty years at Hull-House*. New York: Macmillan.
———. (1964). *Democracy and social ethics* (Scott, A. F., Ed.). Cambridge, MA: Harvard University.

———. (1965). *The social thought of Jane Addams*. (Lasch, C., Ed.). New York: Bobbs-Merrill.
Downs, R. B. (1974). *Books that changed America*. New York: Macmillan.

SELECTED OTHER WORKS BY JANE ADDAMS

A centennial reader. (1930). (E. C. Johnson, Ed.). New York: Macmillan.
Jane Addams on peace, war and international understanding, 1899–1932. (1976). (A. F. Davis, Ed.). New York: Garland.

SELECTED OTHER WORKS ABOUT JANE ADDAMS

Davis, A. F. (1973). *American heroine: Life and legend of Jane Addams*. New York: Oxford University Press.
Farrell, J. (1967). *Beloved lady: History of Jane Addams' ideas on reform and peace*. Baltimore, MD: Johns Hopkins Press.
Hovde, J. (1989). *Jane Addams*. New York: Facts on File.
Levine, D. (1971). *Jane Addams and the liberal tradition*. Madison: State Historical Society of Wisconsin.
Linn, J. W. (1935). *Jane Addams: A biography*. New York: Appleton-Century.
Tims, M. (1961). *Jane Addams of Hull-House*. New York: Macmillan.
Wise, W. E. (1935). *Jane Addams of Hull-House*. New York: Harcourt, Brace.

6

Maria Montessori: Educating Children for Independence

Maria Montessori was an Italian and most of her work was done in Europe and India, but her influence on U.S. schools has been substantial. The first woman in Italy to obtain a medical degree, Dr. Montessori first became interested in education through her psychological research with children with mental disabilities. After achieving success teaching them to read and write via her scientifically designed materials, she turned her energies to teaching normal children in public schools with the same strategies, known as the "Montessori Method."

In the early 1900s, Montessori came several times to America to speak about, publicize, and demonstrate her philosophy. She was well received by many teachers and parents who wanted an experimental approach to childhood education, but was also criticized by some of the leaders in the American progressive movement that was also taking hold at the time, at least in private schools. The goal of both was to develop the potential of individual children and to encourage social interaction, but they differed in some significant ways.

For a variety of reasons, Montessori schools mostly died out for several decades in the United States, but were revived during the

1960s. Today, many such schools flourish at the preschool and elementary levels, although not exactly as originally designed. These schools are favored by those who want children to practice self-discipline, independent thought and action, and cooperative living.

EARLY YEARS

In 1870, the same year that Italy separated from Austria and became a unified country, Maria Montessori was born in a small village. Like all countries changing quickly to industrialization, Italy was overwhelmed with social problems—slums, poor sanitation, abysmal working conditions, and low wages. Men, women, and children labored twelve or more hours a day in factories, water-filled rice fields, or sulfur mines. The Montessori family later moved to Rome where enlightenment thought was producing a strong social consciousness, and efforts were being made to rid the country of oppression, poverty, and illiteracy. However, the reform movement soon waned. Twenty years later, most Italians were still destitute and uneducated. Child labor was common and corruption in government rife.

Maria's father, a civil servant, had conventional ideas about how to raise his only child, but her mother, the niece of a famous scholar-priest, encouraged the girl to uncommon educational and career aspirations. She also insisted that Maria learn about the plight of poor families and gave her such tasks as scrubbing tile floors and taking a hunchbacked girl for walks. These lessons were later reflected in Montessori's emphasis on "exercises in practical living" and in treating all labors and all children with respect, no matter what their status or physical and mental capacities.

Maria attended a crowded, dirty elementary school in Rome, staffed with untrained, poorly educated teachers. Despite this, she developed a love for mathematics and later insisted on enrolling in the technical rather than the college preparation school. In an age when females were not permitted to go into the streets alone, she was amazingly independent. Unfortunately, however, the secondary school was no better than the primary. Learning was by drill, students studied the same material at the same pace, and nothing was ever discussed. Boys and girls were segregated, even on the playground.

After graduation, Maria studied mathematics and science at the University of Rome and then decided to enter medical school, even though women were barred from enrollment. Determined, she cajoled officials, perhaps even the Pope, until she was admitted. Once there, however, she had to be escorted to class by her disapproving father, wait until all males were seated before entering, dissect cadavers alone in the evenings, and withstand the disdain and hostility of faculty and students.

Eventually, through her outstanding scholastic performance, seriousness of purpose, and good humor, she earned the respect of professors and fellow students. In 1896, she earned her degree and won several coveted awards. Displaying high energy, she became a surgical assistant at the university-connected hospital, worked part time at the children's and women's hospitals, and started her own private practice.

Because publicity accompanied her graduation from medical school (she was called the "beautiful scholar"), Montessori was courted by wealthy women in Rome and invited to give public talks. Poised and charismatic, she often spoke out for the rights of the oppressed and sought donations for social action projects. At age twenty-six, she addressed the International Congress of Women in Berlin as Italy's official representative.

According to biographer Rita Kramer, Montessori never married, but had an affair with a fellow psychiatrist that resulted in a son, Mario. Because the knowledge of this would have wrecked her career, she secretly placed the baby with a country family and later in a boarding school until his adolescence. Mario Montessori was thrilled as a youth to discover his real mother was the famous doctor and educator. When grown, he became a devoted disciple and fellow researcher, whom she passed off as a nephew or adopted son until late in her life.

Initially, Dr. Montessori had no desire to be a teacher, the normal and often the only career for educated women, but soon became drawn into the profession by her interest in science. Memories of her poor public education and her work with mentally disabled children led her to research how children develop physically, morally, and intellectually. From her discoveries came a radically new approach to education.

FROM INSANE ASYLUM TO CASA DEI BAMBINI

Along with her medical work, Montessori conducted studies at the psychiatric clinic at the University of Rome and made frequent visits to what were known as insane asylums. She was distressed to discover children placed there who were not mentally ill but were mentally handicapped. Having nothing to play with or do, the children sat and stared at the walls. Montessori read all she could find on mental retardation, particularly Jean Itard's work (1801) with a deaf-mute boy discovered living alone in the wild, and brought some children to her clinic for observation. Certain that they could be helped, not in asylums but in schools, she turned her attention to education.

Of the major education philosophers, she was most impressed by Jean Jacques Rousseau, Johann Pestalozzi, and Friedrich Froebel because of their humanistic emphasis on the worth of the individual, the importance of early childhood education, and the need to develop the senses.

Montessori then devoted her energy to establishing special schools for children previously deemed uneducable. Claiming that all persons are capable of learning—an extreme view at the time— and arguing that juvenile delinquency stems from a bad environment, not from inherited defects, her lectures, writings, and newspaper publicity had an impact on the public. By age thirty, she was well known in Italy and received many awards for outstanding service.

In 1906, when Montessori was thirty-six and highly regarded as a scientist and educator, she was asked to help with an urban renewal project sponsored by some wealthy bankers. They had renovated an empty apartment complex to house Rome's poorest families, only to find it defaced by fifty unsupervised preschool children. Her task was to organize a nursery any way she wished. Although her colleagues thought it foolish for a well-known educator to undertake such a lowly project, she saw it as an opportunity to try out her ideas on normal children. She collected funds for materials and toys from wealthy friends and hired several women in the complex to run the program. Within three months, the children turned from unruly, fearful individuals into disciplined, happy, confident ones.

Publicity about her success at Casa dei Bambini brought visitors from all over the world, and a group of devoted disciples surrounded her. Similar schools were set up, and eventually her methods became the established system for Italy and Switzerland's public schools and spread to other European countries and

America. Because of this international success, Montessori gave up her medical practice and devoted the rest of her life to promoting her methods, writing books, establishing schools, and training teachers. From her work with mentally disabled and poor children came an educational philosophy radically different from the passive, dehumanizing methods found in most schools in Italy and elsewhere at the time.

THE MONTESSORI PHILOSOPHY

The fundamental principle of the Montessori Method is to give children the freedom to teach themselves. Montessori believed that a child's spontaneous desire to learn should not be hindered by a teacher's wish to control. By doing things for themselves, children become self-reliant, exhibit self-worth, respect others, and are motivated to learn the rest of their lives.

"To stimulate life,—leaving it then free to develop, to unfold," she wrote, is the "first task of the educator" (1912, 115).

Schools, said Montessori, should be places where pupils can freely develop their abilities, not simply do tasks assigned by an adult. It is not "teaching" that helps a child grow, but a prepared, stimulating environment in which a child can explore and practice. The stress should be on independence, practicality and self-control. All learning should have application for everyday life—caring for oneself and achieving good social relations with others. "The first educational influence upon a child," she wrote, "should have as its object the guidance of the child along the way of independence. No one can be free if he is not independent" (1967b, 57).

While observing the children at Casa dei Bambini, Montessori learned some surprising things. First of all, the three- and four-year-olds spurned the toys in favor of the self-correcting materials she had designed for mentally disabled children. They consistently chose problem-solving objects like puzzles and games over dolls and tea sets. Montessori perceived this as a desire on the part of youngsters to do sensible tasks, real jobs. She encouraged parents to have their children work alongside them in their homes, doing whatever chores they could. In her classrooms, the pupils dusted, swept floors, arranged flowers, watered plants, prepared and served food, and washed dishes. These occupations, which they did with pride, gave them a sense of ownership and control. They were not interested in rewards, but worked for the pleasure of completing tasks.

Sensitive Periods

A major Montessori contribution to educational philosophy, later developed further by Swiss psychologist Jean Piaget, was the idea of "sensitive periods" in children's lives when certain skills and attitudes are easily acquired. If a period passes unfulfilled, the child will never later approach the task with the same eagerness. A desire by preschoolers for order in the environment is one such sensitive period. They find chaos painful, Montessori noted, and take delight in putting objects precisely in place—a desire that parents and schools should encourage and appreciate.

If a child does not spontaneously choose an activity and become engrossed in it for a period of time, the classroom is at fault, not the child. Children are born explorers. They learn an enormous amount on their own before they start school. Apathy and disruptive behavior arise from the lack of opportunity to make discoveries for themselves.

Once a room was set up with proper materials, the directress's task was to record observations, like "an astronomer who sits fixed at his telescope while the planets go spinning around" (1967b, 51). The directress was instructed to use simple, direct, exact language, keeping talk to a minimum, and to remain passive at all times so that children would interact with the materials and with each other. They would thus learn to correct their own mistakes and control their behavior through natural consequences. Montessori stressed that time and much patience was required of the teacher. When an adult picks up a child struggling to climb stairs, for instance, he or she destroys the excitement, challenge, and sense of achievement. How would a mountain climber like it, she asked, if a giant came along and lifted him to the top?

In contrast to traditional teachers, a Montessori directress was removed from center stage. She was a facilitator, not a lecturer or leader. Once directions were quietly given in as few words as possible, each child was left alone, with the adult watching for problems and observing growth. Children were allowed to carry their chosen objects to wherever they wished in the classroom—to a table or a small carpet spread on the floor—and spend as much time as they liked. The directress watched that no one took a desired object from another child, interfered with another's work, or used the materials incorrectly. Although children could choose which materials to manipulate, they were required to use them only for their designed purpose.

The aim of a teacher in a regular school was to teach as much as she could. The aim of a Montessori directress was to teach as little as possible and let the children learn by themselves from the prepared environment. *"The essential thing is for the task to arouse such an interest that it engages the child's whole personality,"* she stated (1967a, 206). Once that happens, the child should not be helped nor interrupted, for both destroy concentration and enjoyment. "The child who concentrates is immensely happy. . . . *As soon as concentration has begun, act as if the child does not exist"* (1967a, 272, 280).

Child-Centered, Scientific, and Relevant

Given today's rhetoric about child-centered education, it is sometimes difficult to realize that in Montessori's day this was a revolutionary philosophy. In a typical school, furniture was built for adults, teachers were poorly trained, and the instructional method was memorization and drill. All decisions were made by the teacher and little effort was given to discover how children learned or what their needs or interests were. Furthermore, what learning did occur was unrelated to the child's everyday life.

Montessori's first innovation was to design facilities in her classrooms so children could wash their hands and dishes, put equipment away on low shelves, and sit on child-size chairs at low, light weight, movable tables. She abhorred desks! From her psychiatrist and physician point of view, desks stunted the spirit and curved the spine. Each day the children prepared a nutritious lunch and served it to each other. The directress and aides were nearby if needed, but the three- to five-year-olds did the work enthusiastically by themselves. Montessori considered these "exercises in practical living" a very important part of her educational philosophy, for they taught children to be masters of their environment.

Unlike other schools, children were not segregated by either age or gender and both girls and boys participated in all domestic tasks: "To segregate by age is one of the cruelest and most inhuman things one can do. . . . It breaks the bonds of social life, deprives it of nourishment. . . . It is an artificial isolation and impedes the development of the social sense" (1967a, 226). The children washed and dressed themselves, put materials away, cleaned the rooms, and grew vegetables in a garden for their lunches.

A second important aspect of the Montessori schooling was motor education. The children participated in daily gymnastics and rhythmic exercises. For large muscle development, she invented the parallel bars used in today's gym classes. To exercise small muscles, children worked with modeling clay, hooks, buttons, laces, and strings of beads. These seem like normal activities today, but in the early 1900s they were unique and were perceived by many critics as a "waste of time."

The third part of the Montessori Method involved intellectual and sense development. While working with mentally disabled children, Montessori designed a set of materials to teach skills needed for academic achievement. She discovered which items children found most interesting and modified her designs accordingly. Determining the suitability by asking the children what they preferred was itself a novel approach to education (and still is in many classrooms).

To help students see distinctions, Montessori created wooden cylinders for different size holes, cubes of decreasing size to build a tower, and prisms and rods for stair-building. Using these, the child indirectly learned about precision and geometry. A series of colored tablets taught gradation of colors. The materials were all self-correcting, showing immediate, tangible results, so that error was controlled by the objects and not by the teacher—thus eliminating human judgment and criticism. Today, we buy plastic versions of these "educational toys" in department stores, not knowing who was their inventor.

Montessori maintained that the "sensitive period" for learning to write is about four years old—earlier than usually believed—and that writing should precede reading. Once again, she developed her materials while working with children of low intelligence, but found them equally suitable for normal students. Wanting something that was both cheap and tactile, she cut out large paper letters, glued on sandpaper so the children could feel as well as see, and pasted them on wooden blocks for a three-dimensional effect. Children moved rapidly from touching the letters, to writing words on the chalkboard, to composing notes to each other, and finally to reading books.

She also believed that reading should be done silently, for meaning, because reading aloud involves the additional skill of elocution and is a more difficult task. From the moment her children began to write (having been prepared by practicing hand and arm movements with a slim rod), they moved to reading on an average of fifteen days.

DISCIPLINE METHODS

Like the later Behaviorists, such as B. F. Skinner, Montessori believed that the environment is a major influence on one's actions. Problems are not innate in a child, she stated, but occur in classrooms where children are engaged in "useless play" rather than "meaningful work." When children are allowed to choose from a variety of instructive and interesting tasks, can spend as much time as they wish, and do not have their attention interrupted by others, behavior problems seldom arise. Self-discipline naturally follows absorption in a project.

Although generally the directress and aides were to remain passive and not interfere with children's work, Montessori did recognize the need for a few rules of conduct. First of all, pupils were forbidden to abuse the materials or use them in ways not intended. Obviously, destructive behavior could not be condoned, and because the materials were designed for self-correction, a child could attain the objective only from their proper use. For instance, if the task was to place round shapes into round holes and square ones into square holes, a child who stacked the shapes in a column or rolled them on the floor was not learning the task.

Second, the children were not allowed to hurt each other or interfere with another's work. One pupil could invite another to share the same equipment, but neither was permitted to demand a turn or grab the materials. Enough objects were provided in the classroom so that children could freely choose what they wished to work with and could stay with the activity as long as they desired. The directress handled any breaking of rules in a swift, objective, low-toned, nonjudgmental manner.

When a child first entered a Montessori classroom, which could be done at any time of the year, problems sometimes resulted until the child adjusted to rules and expectations. When necessary, an adult moved a disruptive child to an isolated spot in order to protect the others. The child was placed, however, so that he or she could see the other children happily at work and was allowed to return at any time. Montessori suggested treating such children as if they were ill, catering to them as one does a sick child. This attitude stressed the point that self-discipline and work is the normal state of a happy child and anyone who deviates must be temporarily ill and in need of care. Because children prefer to be healthy and treated alike, the catered-to child is pitied rather than envied and soon wants nothing better than to join classmates in meaningful activity.

Of utmost importance, said Montessori, is lack of either punishment or rewards as a means of discipline. Adults should neither chastise nor praise children, for punishment robs them of self-respect and praise robs them of the confidence to judge the worth of their own work. "To tell a person he is clever or clumsy, bright, stupid, good or bad, is a form of betrayal. The child must see for himself what he can do" (1967a, 250). Because the Montessori tasks were self-correcting, children learned by trial and error if they had succeeded and did not need an adult to tell them so. "Things are the best teachers," she proclaimed (Kramer, 261), and the crux of her philosophy was that children learn best by themselves from a specially prepared environment and are hindered by adult attempts to teach and control.

MONTESSORI IN AMERICA: THE CRITICS

In the early 1900s, after the Montessori Method was officially adopted in public schools in Italy and Switzerland, scores of articles appeared in U.S. journals. Among the hundreds who traveled to Italy to observe her methods were prominent U.S. educators and psychologists like Jane Addams, Arnold and Beatrice Gesell, and G. Stanley Hall.

The first U.S. Montessori school, begun in 1911, was a much publicized small private institution for well-to-do children in Tarrytown, New York. Another was established in Washington, DC, for the grandchildren of Alexander Graham Bell. In 1913, a Montessori Education Association was formed. Montessori made several trips at this time to America, including a triumphal visit to the International Exposition in California in 1915. She held classes in a glass building with bleachers outside for an audience that was amazed at the attention span of children engrossed in her materials.

Some Americans, however, were critical of her methods. Besides the traditionalists, who objected to the idea of children having the right to choose their tasks and control their time, several prominent progressive educators raised serious concerns. William Kilpatrick, dean of education at Columbia University who was a disciple of John Dewey, wrote in 1914 that her methods were "fifty years behind present development of educational theory" (63). He particularly objected to the lack of creative activities and viewed her method as a restrictive, mechanical approach to education, allowing for little social interplay and variety and no imagination. With her technological and scientific background, Montessori had no interest in the arts. She believed fairy tales, for instance, to be a dangerous distraction from, and not nearly as interesting as factual information about the real world.

After World War I, Montessori schools lost favor in the United States. Besides the criticism of educators, other factors figured significantly in this decline: America's involvement against Italy in two world wars, prejudice toward Italian immigrants who were flooding the cities, lack of esteem for female scholars, antagonism toward feminist leaders, the requirement that Montessori teachers be trained only in Italy, the belief that young children belonged at home and not in preschools, and the conviction by psychologists that intelligence was fixed at birth and could not be altered by the environment.

In the 1960s, however, an interest in Montessori schooling re-emerged in America. Early education and independent learning were once again in vogue. Researchers such as Erik Erikson and Jean Piaget, both of whom were influenced by Montessorian ideas, were having an impact on educational psychology. Sensitive to the charge of ignoring creativity and the imagination, Montessori schools in more recent times, especially in the United States, incorporated art, music, drama, and dance into the typical program, and thus became more acceptable to educators and parents who want an emphasis on the arts in education.

LATER YEARS AND LASTING ACHIEVEMENTS

Because of her opposition to World War I, Montessori and her philosophy were unwelcome for a while in Italy, so she lived those years in the United States and Spain. Ironically, in 1924 she convinced the dictator Mussolini, not one to encourage independent thought, to re-instate her methods in Italian public schools. In Germany in the 1930s, however, all her schools were ordered closed and her effigy was burned in Berlin. Soon after, Montessori schools were also shut down in Austria and again in Italy.

In 1939, at age sixty-nine, Montessori went to India to give a teacher-training course. Because of the enthusiastic reception, she stayed for seven years, meeting Mohatma Ghandi and Jawaharial Nehru, and worked toward alleviating the immense problems of poverty and illiteracy. While there, she was three times nominated for, but never received, the Nobel Peace Prize. During World War II, Montessori schools foundered in most of Europe, but in 1947 at the age of seventy-six she was invited to Italy once again to re-organize the public schools according to her system. She returned to India a few years later, then moved to The Netherlands to be near her son Mario and his family. Dr. Maria Montessori died in 1952 at age eighty-one and was buried in a Catholic church cemetery in Noordwijk.

Although the Montessori Method, as originally designed, limited the freedom of students to the structured environment prepared by the directress and included few of the arts, the emphasis on individual interests and independent thought was a precursor of modern Constructivist philosophy and related reforms.

Excerpts from Maria Montessori

In her book, *The Montessori Method*, translated into English by Anne George in 1912, Montessori severely criticized the method used to teach writing in the Italian schools and described her scientific approach for designing appropriate materials, which she first used successfully with mentally disabled children. She also castigated those who made simple things complicated and started with preconceived ideas about how children ought to learn, rather than observing how they actually do learn.

Even we in these days still believe that in order to learn to write the child must first make vertical strokes. This conviction is very general. Yet it does not seem natural that to write the letters of the alphabet, which are all rounded, it should be necessary to begin with straight lines and acute angles.

In all good faith, we wonder that it should be difficult to do away with the angularity and stiffness with which the beginner traces the beautiful curve of the 0. Yet, through what effort on our part, and on his, was he forced to fill pages and pages with rigid lines and acute angles! To whom is due this time-honored idea that the first sign to be traced must be a straight line? And why do we so avoid preparing for curves as well as angles?

Let us, for a moment, divest ourselves of such preconceptions and proceed in a more simple way. We may be able to relieve future generations of *all effort* in the matter of learning to write.

Is it necessary to begin writing with the making of vertical strokes? A moment of clear and logical thinking is enough to enable us to answer, no. The child makes too painful an effort in following such an exercise. The first steps should be the easiest, and the up and down stroke, is, on the contrary, one of the most difficult of all the pen movements. Only a professional penman could fill a whole page and preserve the regularity of such strokes. . . . In the methods ordinarily used in teaching writing, we add . . . the further restriction that the instrument of writing must be held in a certain way, not as instinct prompts each individual.

Thus we approach in the most conscious and restricted way the first act of writing, which should be voluntary. In this first writing we still demand that the single strokes be kept parallel, making the child's task a difficult and barren one, since it has no purpose for the child, who does not understand the meaning of all this detail. . . . That vertical strokes should prepare for alphabetical writing, seems incredibly illogical. The alphabet is made up of curves, therefore we must prepare for it by learning to make straight lines (256–259). . . .

Let us observe an individual who is writing, and let us seek to analyze the acts he performs in writing, that is, the mechanical operations which enter into the execution of writing. . . . it goes without saying that we should examine the individual who writes, not the *writing;* the *subject,* not the *object* . . . a method starting from the individual would be decidedly original—very different from other methods which preceded it. It would indeed signify a new era in writing, *based upon anthropology* . . . which seems to me the natural one, the method of *spontaneous* writing (260).

After observing a child with mental disabilities fail at the task of sewing, unable to weave a needle in and out of the material, Montessori gave her a hand-sized loom in which a strip of paper was threaded in and out among vertical strips of paper fixed at the top and bottom. After she became skilled at this, the girl was able to do darning with little trouble. Montessori took this principle of learning a difficult task by first mastering a similar but easier one and applied it to the teaching of writing.

I had a beautiful alphabet manufactured, the letters being in flowing script. . . . These letters were in wood, ½ centimeter in thickness, and were painted, the consonants in blue enamel, the vowels in red. The underside of these letter forms, instead of being painted, were covered with bronze that they might be more durable. We had only one copy of this wooden alphabet; but there were a number of cards upon which the letters were painted in the same colors and dimensions as the wooden ones. . . . Corresponding to each letter of the alphabet, we had a picture representing some object the name of which began with the letter . . . to fix the memory of the sound of the letter. . . .

The interesting part of my experiment was, that after I had shown the children how to place the movable wooden letters upon those painted in groups upon the cards, I had them *touch them repeatedly in the fashion of flowing writing.*

I multiplied these exercises in various ways, and the children thus learned to make *the movements necessary to reproduce the form of the graphic signs without writing.*

I was struck by an idea which had never before entered my mind—that in writing we make *two diverse* forms of movement, for, besides the movement by which the form is reproduced, there is also that of *manipulating the instrument of writing.* And, indeed, when the deficient children had become expert in touching all the letters according to form, *they did not yet know how to hold a pencil.* To hold and to manipulate a little stick securely, corresponds to the *acquisition of a special muscular mechanism which is independent of the writing movement;* it must in fact go along with the motions necessary to produce all of the various letter forms. It is, then, *a distinct mechanism,* which must exist together with the motor memory of the single graphic signs (261–263).

Montessori then added a second movement for the children to do repeatedly that would prepare them for the muscular mechanism necessary for using a pencil as well as for writing letters. They traced the letters on the blocks or cards with their index and middle fingers, then traced them again with a little wooden stick, holding it between their fingers like a pencil. In this way, they learned both the shapes of letters and how to manipulate a writing instrument. By using her scientific method of observation with the special needs children with which she first worked, Montessori came to the conclusion that learning to write should precede learning to read—that writing came much more easily to children.

It was with great surprise that I noted the *facility* with which a deficient child, to whom I one day gave a piece of chalk, traced upon the blackboard, in a firm hand, the letters of the entire alphabet, writing for the first time.

This had arrived much more quickly than I had supposed. As I have said, some of the children wrote the letters *with a pen and yet could not recognize one of them*. I have noticed, also, in normal children, that the muscular sense is most easily developed in infancy, and this makes writing exceedingly easy for children. It is not so with reading, which requires a much longer course of instruction, and which calls for a superior intellectual development, since it treats of the *interpretation of signs*, and of the *modulation of accents of the voice*, in order that the word may be understood. And all this is a purely mental task, while in writing, the child, under dictation, *materially translates* sounds into signs, and *moves*, a thing which is always easy and pleasant for him. Writing develops in the little child with *facility* and *spontaneity*, analogous to the development of spoken language. . . . Reading, on the contrary, makes part of an abstract intellectual culture, which is the interpretation of ideas from graphic symbols, and is only acquired later on (266–267).

> Montessori took her new ideas to Casa dei Bambini, the preschool in Rome, where she was asked to bring discipline to poorly cared for and unruly children of normal intelligence. She wanted to compare their progress in learning to write, using her method, with children in the public schools. Unable to find anyone to reproduce the wooden blocks, she hit upon a simpler, cheaper idea.

I then decided to cut out large paper letters, and to have one of my teachers color these roughly on one side with a blue tint. As for the touching of the letters, I thought of cutting the letters of the alphabet out of sandpaper, and of gluing them upon smooth cards, thus making objects much like those used in the primitive exercises for the tactile sense.

Only after I had made these simple things, did I become aware of the superiority of this alphabet to that magnificent one I had used for my [special needs children] . . . I finally understood that a paper alphabet could easily be multiplied, and could be used by many children at one time, not only for the recognition of letters, but for the composition of words. I saw that in the sandpaper alphabet I had found the looked-for guide for the fingers which touched the letter. This was furnished in such a way that no longer the sight alone, but the touch, lent itself directly to teaching the movement of writing with exactness of control (268–269).

> An important modification was later made by an instructor in the teacher-training school. She placed a strip of white paper behind each letter to indicate the direction because children often turned them upside down or sideways. She also built simple cardboard cases so that each letter could be neatly placed in its own compartment. Montessori not only appreciated these additions, but was gratified by the children's pleasure working with the sandpaper letters and by their progress.

Less than a month and a half later, while the children in the first elementary [in public school] were laboriously working to forget their wearisome pothooks [straight lines and angles] and to prepare for making the curves of 0 and the other vowels, two of my little ones of four years old, wrote, each one in the name of his companions, a letter of good wishes and thanks to [the Director General who helped establish the tenement school] . . . upon note paper without blot or erasure and the writing was adjudged equal to that which is obtained in the third elementary grade (270).

> An essential element in Montessori's method is teaching for independence. Children, she noted, from the moment they are weaned are striving toward this. The purpose of schooling should be to guide them in ways that allow for individuality and taking responsibility for themselves within a social, supportive context.

Any pedagogical action, if it is to be efficacious in the training of little children, must tend to *help* the children to advance upon this road of independence. We must help them to learn to walk without assistance, to run, to go up and down stairs, to lift up fallen objects, to dress and undress themselves, to bathe themselves, to speak distinctly, and to express their own needs clearly. We must give such help as shall make it possible for children to achieve the satisfaction of their own individual aims and desires. All this is a part of education for independence.

We habitually *serve* children; and this is not only an act of servility toward them, but it is dangerous, since it tends to suffocate their useful, spontaneous activity. We are inclined to believe that children are like puppets, and we wash them and feed them as if they were dolls. We do not stop to think that the child *who does not do, does not know how to do* . . . our duty toward him is, in every case, that of *helping him* to make a conquest of such useful acts as nature intended he should perform for himself (97–98).

> Montessori, like some more recent psychologists, believed that children should be given neither prizes nor punishments for their behavior.

One day I took with me on a visit [to the tenement school] a lady who praised the children highly and who, opening a box she had brought, showed them a number of shining medals, each tied with a bright red ribbon. "The mistress," she said, "will put these on the breasts of those children who are the cleverest and the best."

As I was under no obligation to instruct this visitor in my methods, I kept silence, and the teacher took the box. At that moment, a most intelligent little boy of four, who was seated quietly at one of the little tables, wrinkled his forehead in an act of protest and cried out over and over again;—"Not to the boys, though, not to the boys!"

What a revelation! This little fellow already knew that he stood among the best and strongest of his class, although no one had ever revealed this fact to him, and he did not wish to be offended by this prize. Not knowing how to defend his dignity, he invoked the superior quality of his masculinity!

As to punishments, we have many times come in contact with children who disturbed the others without paying any attention to our corrections. Such children were at once examined by the phy-sician. When the case proved to be that of a normal child, we placed one of the little tables in a corner of the room, and in this way iso-lated the child; having him sit in a comfortable little armchair, so placed that he might see his companions at work, and giving him those games and toys to which he was most attracted. This isola-tion almost always succeeded in calming the child; from his posi-tion he could see the entire assembly of his companions, and the way in which they carried on their work was an *object lesson* much more efficacious than any words of the teacher could possibly have been. Little by little, he would come to see the advantages of being one of the company working so busily before his eyes, and he would really wish to go back and do as the others did. . . .

The isolated child was always made the object of special care, almost as if he were ill. I myself, when I entered the room, went first of all directly to him, caressing him, as if he were a very little child. Then I turned my attention to the others, interesting myself in their work, asking questions about it as if they had been little men. I do not know what happened in the soul of these children whom we found it necessary to discipline, but certainly the conversion was always very complete and lasting. They showed great pride in learning how to work and how to conduct themselves, and always showed a very tender affection for the teacher and for me (102–104).

> Montessori's graduate studies and research in psychology were applied to the teaching of young children, which she consid-ered to be the most interesting, important, and rewarding of careers. Yet she recognized that much more needed to be known about how children develop and learn.

In regard to infant psychology, we are more richly endowed with prejudices than with actual knowledge bearing upon the subject. We have, until the present day, wished to dominate the child through force, by the imposition of external laws, instead of mak-ing an interior conquest of the child, in order to direct him as a human soul. In this way, the children have lived beside us without being able to make us know them. But if we cut away the artifici-ality with which we have enwrapped them, and the violence through which we have foolishly thought to discipline them, they will reveal themselves to us in all the truth of child nature.

Their gentleness is so absolute, so sweet, that we recognize in it the infancy of that humanity which can remain oppressed by every form of yoke, by every injustice; and the child's love of *knowledge* is such that it surpasses every other love (117–118).

REFERENCES

Kilpatrick, W. H. (1914). *The Montessori system examined.* Boston: Houghton Mifflin. Reprint, New York: Arno Press & the *New York Times*, 1971.

Kramer, R. (1976). *Maria Montessori: A biography.* New York: G. P. Putnam's Sons.

Montessori, M. (1912). *The Montessori method* (George, A. E., Trans.). New York: Fredrick A. Stokes.

———. (1967a). *The absorbent mind* (Claremont, C., Trans.). New York: Dell. (First published in 1949).

———. (1967b). *The discovery of the child* (Costelloe, M. J., Trans.) Notre Dame, IN: Fides. (First published in 1948).

SELECTED OTHER WORKS BY MARIA MONTESSORI

Education for a new world. (1946). Adyar, India: Kalakshetra.

To educate the human potential (1948). Adyar, India: Kalakshetra.

The secret of childhood (1972). New York: Ballantine Books. (First published in 1936).

SELECTED OTHER WORKS ABOUT MARIA MONTESSORI

Hainstock, E. G. (1997). *The essential Montessori.* New York: Plume.

Lillard, P. P. (1972). *Montessori: A modern approach.* New York: Schocken.

Montessori, M. M. (1992). *Education for human development: Understanding Montessori.* Oxford: Clio. (Author is Maria Montessori's son, Mario).

Shephard, M. T. (1996). *Maria Montessori: Teacher of teachers.* Minneapolis: Lerner.

Standing, E. M. (1962). *Maria Montessori: Her life and work.* New York: The New American Library of World Literature. (First published in 1917).

Wentworth, R.A.L. (1999). *Montessori for the millennium.* Mahwah, NJ: L. Erlbaum Assoc.

7

Mary McLeod Bethune: Educating African-American Youth

In the 1940s, two of the most distinguished women in America were good friends of different races: First Lady Eleanor Roosevelt and Mary McLeod Bethune. A child of illiterate, freed slaves in South Carolina, Bethune had become a college president and a national leader in education, justice, and world peace.

Despite her prodigious accomplishments and international reputation, Mary Bethune has been overlooked by most historians of education. Although textbooks are now including more about African Americans, the emphasis is on the education of Black males and the achievements of male leaders such as Frederick Douglass, Booker T. Washington, and W.E.B. DuBois. This awareness, of course, is well deserved, but the amazing work of Mary McLeod Bethune in providing educational opportunities for African-American girls in the south and later for both sexes, plus her life-long efforts to improve the lives of Black Americans everywhere, is also worthy of much recognition.

EARLY YEARS

Mary Jane McLeod was born on a cotton farm in South Carolina in 1875, ten years after the Civil War ended. The fifteenth of seventeen children, she was born free, but her parents and older siblings had all been slaves. Their last name was that of the plantation owner, with whom they maintained a good relationship. Most of the family, including her grandmother, lived in a pine shack and worked as sharecroppers in the same cotton fields after the war. Mary's mother was a proud, skillful, religious woman, said to be of royal African lineage, and her father was a hardworking farmer, carpenter, and leather maker. They were the leaders of their Black community and respected by White neighbors.

Mary, who occasionally played with the White children in the big house on the old plantation, saw their books and was determined to read and write. She would be the first in her family to do so because South Carolina law had forbidden slave literacy. Mary was a precocious child, intelligent, self-confident, and talkative, with a talent for singing. She yearned to go to school, but there were none for African-American children. Instead, her days were spent in the cotton and rice fields until the Presbyterian Mission Board sent a Black teacher to Mayesville, five miles away, to open a small school. Recognizing their young child's potential, Mary's parents enrolled her and with a grateful heart she made the daily ten-mile walk. In the evenings she taught reading and arithmetic to her family and others in the community.

To her great joy, on graduation Mary received a modest scholarship from a White woman in Denver named Mary Chrissman, a Quaker teacher and seamstress who wanted to use her meager savings to help an African-American female get an education. Mary enrolled in Scotia Seminary, a boarding school for Black girls in North Carolina that had an integrated faculty. Seeing educated Black teachers accepted as equals with Whites, she said, removed forever her feelings of inferiority. The school also helped her discover her talents, especially for singing and public speaking. By working at numerous jobs, she was able to stay at the school for seven years, never going home, and earned the equivalent of a junior college degree.

At age nineteen, Mary McLeod was granted another scholarship by Miss Chrissman and entered Moody Bible Institute in Chicago, determined to be a missionary in Africa. At Moody she was the only Black student, but met many students from Japan, China, and India. Although she found no racism at the school, she encountered it after graduation. To her astonishment, the Presbyterian Mission Board refused to send her to work with Black Africans because she was a Black American.

Greatly disappointed, but needing a job, in 1896 she accepted a teaching position at Haines Normal Institute in Augusta, Georgia, founded by a former slave, Lucy Craft Laney. In addition to her daily classes, Mary started a Sunday school for children, both Black and White, who played in the dirty streets and alleys. They were taught Bible stories, cleanliness, and moral behavior and some were organized into a large choral group. A year later, Mary was transferred to Kindell Institute in Sumter, South Carolina. While there she married Albertus Bethune, whom she met in the church choir, and they soon had a son, Albert McLeod Bethune. The following year they moved to Palatka, Florida, where Mary directed the Presbyterian Mission School for the next four years.

DAYTONA BEACH SCHOOL

In 1904, Mary Bethune, at age twenty-nine, opened a school of her own in Daytona Beach, where Black men were laboring for a pittance on a new railroad. Their families were living in squalid conditions, as bad or worse than slavery. Because treatment of slaves before the Civil War had been so cruel in the south, many Whites lived in constant fear of Black revenge. In many places, African Americans were still treated harshly. "Jim Crow laws" segregated all public facilities. Blacks could not eat with White people and were often arrested and beaten for such things as having a "sassy" attitude or for being in a White area after dark. Poll taxes prevented them from voting and the Ku Klux Klan terrorized both Black communities and White sympathizers.

Determined to give to others what Mary Chrissman and her teachers had given her—hope and enough education to rise above oppression—Mary Bethune rented a run-down two-story frame house and, with furniture from the town dump and money begged from door to door, she founded a boarding school named the Daytona Educational and Industrial Training School for Negro Girls, beginning with five young female pupils. Their parents could pay little or nothing and food was often scarce. Crisis followed crisis, but two years later the school had 250 students, an enlarged building, two poorly paid teachers, and several volunteers.

Needing even bigger quarters, Bethune bought a town dump for two hundred dollars (with a five dollar down payment) and began a long-term effort to acquire suitable buildings, furnishings, and school supplies. The girls sold home-grown vegetables, ice cream, and sweet potato pies and sang spirituals at fancy resort hotels. A highly successful singing tour to northern states helped build public relations for the school and raised much needed money.

Additionally, Bethune gave talks at White churches and women's meetings and soon had an enthusiastic following for her enterprise. She organized an interracial board of trustees and cultivated wealthy Whites who vacationed or wintered in the Daytona Beach area, including James Gamble (of Proctor and Gamble), John D. Rockefeller, and Thomas H. White (president of White sewing machines). Although they and others were generous with donations, and sometimes provided large benefits in their wills, expenses for the school constantly outran income. Providing simple food and clothing was a daily problem, so once a week Bethune bicycled through the area begging for offerings. Respected for her work, many residents would set aside a modest sum to give whenever she knocked.

Curriculum and Educational Philosophy

Initially established for grades one through eight, the Daytona school was geared toward girls who had no advantages at home. Many had never seen a toilet or used eating utensils before coming to the school. In addition to reading, writing, and arithmetic, they were taught cleanliness, thrift, sewing, cooking, and pride in work. The motto in the kitchen read: "Cease to be a drudge. Seek to be an artist." Bethune was convinced that book learning was only a small part of education. For poor Black girls, especially, schooling had to meet their unique needs. As future wives and mothers, they would be the key to improving the lives of generations to come. Thus, it was crucial to practice while still in school all of the skills necessary to be good homemakers, workers, and citizens: problem solving, creativity, good work habits, and high standards for domestic duties. The students were responsible not only for academic learning, but for cooking meals, housecleaning, dressmaking, planting and harvesting vegetables, and all other tasks needed in their daily living. Active involvement permeated all that they did.

Eventually, a high school program was added, despite opposition from board members who, like their counterparts in public schools, considered eight grades enough education for Black children. The school grew to four hundred students, mostly boarders from all over the south. Evening classes in reading and writing were offered to illiterate adults who often paid for the lessons by doing painting, woodworking, or sewing for the school.

On Sundays, older students walked three miles to the turpentine camps in Tomoka where destitute families were barely surviving and lawlessness prevailed. The girls sang hymns and talked about the benefits of temperance, hard work, nutrition, and sanitation. They taught the children to read and play games. Five years later, Bethune had a chain of these schools in the south, called the Tomoka Missions, offering three months of schooling each year.

In 1908, the same year that her marriage dissolved, the boarding school's name was changed slightly and began offering vocational courses for boys as well as girls. Like Booker T. Washington, head of Tuskegee Institute in Alabama, Bethune believed that vocational education was the key to success for most African-American young people at the time. Job opportunities for Black people were severely limited, but with skills in useful trades, they would become self-confident, respected, and economically independent. She taught students to respect their labors no matter how menial, to do their tasks with care, and to not feel demeaned by serving others, whether White or Black. As a very dark-skinned woman who dared to break barriers and speak out against injustices, Bethune frequently met racism and sexism, but faced them with patience and dignity instead of anger or resentment. Self-esteem, she insisted, came from within and not from the judgment of others, and hardship and struggle gave one strength and resilience.

Money was a perennial problem, but the school continued to grow. In 1921, courses two years above high school were offered and the name was changed to Daytona Normal and Industrial Institute. By this time, teacher training had become its primary focus. There were no public high schools for Blacks in Florida, so few Black teachers had schooling beyond eighth grade. Thus, the Daytona institution for many years provided a valuable service in preparing better educated African-American teachers for the segregated elementary schools. Two years later, the school merged with a men's college, Cookman Institute, run by the Methodist Episcopal Church North. The final name became Bethune–Cookman College, with Mary McLeod Bethune as president. In 1947, it received full accreditation as a four-year institution.

As the college expanded, more stress was placed on academic programs, but in all their studies Bethune wanted students to be intelligent learners and to apply their knowledge and skills for the betterment of society. She wrote in "My Last Will and Testament" (1955), that "Knowledge is the prime need of the hour . . . the educational level of the Negro population is at its highest point in history. . . . If we continue in this trend, we will be able to rear increasing numbers of strong purposeful men and women, equipped with vision, mental clarity, health and education" (McCluskey & Smith, 53).

Bethune promoted a realistic attitude in her students, for she knew that on entering a White-dominated world they would face difficult challenges. Their education, therefore, could not merely mimic that of White colleges, but had to be different until the hoped-for time when prejudice and discrimination ceased to exist:

> Negro colleges . . . will do far more [than White colleges] and will be able to teach Negroes to function in a real world of their own, recognizing all of its peculiar handicaps.
>
> Training for the field of teaching will be not simply scientific education at its best, but all of this along with a knowledge of how to serve in a hostile environment which presents hurdles that white education knows nothing about. Other branches of training will be treated in the same way until, in a possible future, the Negro college will be merely another American college serving an American whose problems are parallel with those of other Americans. (1932, 64–65).

Her highest goal was to educate students for courageous and responsible choices, moral ambition, compassionate service, harmonious living, and racial dignity:

> Our children must never lose their zeal for building a better world. They must not be discouraged from aspiring toward greatness, for they are to be the leaders of tomorrow. Nor must they forget that the masses of our people are still underprivileged, ill-housed, impoverished and victimized by discrimination. . . . Faith, courage, brotherhood, dignity, ambition, responsibility—these are needed today as never before. (McCluskey & Smith, 55)

The emphasis of Bethune's educational philosophy was on training the "mind, heart and hand" (1910–1911, 2). This is most clearly summed up by the motto carved in 1914 over the door of the college's administration building: "Enter to learn. Leave to serve."

CRITICS

Like Booker T. Washington, Bethune was criticized in her own time as well as later for stressing domestic and vocational training for Black youths rather than raising their sights toward professional careers. Both of these educators, however, had practical goals. Emancipation was only several decades old when they began their schools. Above all, they wanted their students, most of them children or grandchildren of former slaves, to be economically independent, to gain the self-confidence and pride that comes from earning one's way. Removing the "slave mentality," even in free-born children, was psychologically difficult, especially when laws forbade integration, White society was often cruel, and governments offered little education or other help. In southern states, the only jobs open to Blacks were in service and manual labor. Bethune believed that if her students did these tasks well, they would earn the respect of Whites and be able to move into better paying positions. There was no such thing as menial work, she often said, but only a menial spirit. She believed that gradualism, friendliness, and self-reliance were better antidotes to discrimination and prejudice than militancy or aggressiveness that moved people beyond their readiness to handle challenges and barriers.

Second, both Bethune and Washington were sharply criticized by educated, elite African Americans for hobnobbing with White leaders, toadying wealthy industrialists and playing on their sympathies to get money for their schools. Again, Bethune was pragmatic. She desperately needed funds to house, feed, and educate her students and the only place to obtain the amounts she needed was from well-to-do Whites. Black people had little money to give and many of her girls came from poor families who could pay nothing for tuition. She felt no humiliation in asking for donations, for she believed African Americans deserved the money because of past oppressions, and her school deserved it because of the good that was accomplished in helping students improve their lives and opportunities.

Furthermore, she genuinely liked the Roosevelts, Gambles, Whites, Fields, Rockefellers, Astors, and others who supported her efforts—and they liked her. Confident in the value of her work, she felt in no way demeaned by asking for money and was truly grateful for their interest and generosity. Without their gifts, the school could never have survived and grown. In turn, the donors were highly impressed by her determination, energy, fearlessness, patience, and dignified courtesy even in the face of disrespect and blatant bigotry. Bethune showed no animosity toward Whites or males, despite racial and sexual oppression, and she charmed individuals and audiences by her good humor and congeniality. Being the only African American at a national conference or the first woman appointee fazed her not at all. She was always herself— comfortable, confident, jovial, and proud.

Always an activist for minority rights and opportunities, Bethune encouraged African-American workers to form unions and marched with them in labor protests against discrimination. Because of her membership in a number of organizations that in the 1950s were on the U.S. attorney general's subversive list, she was questioned by the FBI and the House on un-American Activities Committee (HUAC), which caused a storm of protest from religious leaders and other supporters. A very popular public speaker, only once was Bethune refused a platform—by the women's auxiliary of the American Legion in Englewood, New Jersey, because of her "communist leanings." However, her scheduled talk was moved to the local Presbyterian Church and fully attended.

LATER YEARS AND LASTING ACHIEVEMENTS

Besides her extraordinary work for the Daytona school and Bethune–Cookman College, Mary McLeod Bethune contributed greatly to society at large. There were no hospitals for African Americans in Daytona, Florida. When one of her students developed appendicitis, she begged a White doctor to admit the child and operate. He agreed, but placed her in a bed behind the kitchen away from White patients, where she was ill cared for. Immediately, Bethune wrote to all who had previously given to her school (she kept records of even twenty-five cent donations) asking for money to establish a hospital for Black people on her school grounds. In 1911, the McLeod Hospital, named for her parents, opened with two beds. With help from benefactors, this soon grew to a twenty-six-bed institution, staffed by both Black and White doctors. Eventually, a training school for nurses was added. The hospital existed for twenty years until Daytona finally established a hospital for African Americans (still segregated) connected to the city hospital.

Because of her persuasive speaking talents, Mary Bethune was appointed to the American Red Cross in 1914, recruiting Blacks and raising funds. Placed in charge of the Florida chapter, she organized the massive assistance needed when a 1928 hurricane swept through the Everglades area worked by migrant labor.

Bethune had always longed to travel abroad, so a group of devoted friends collected money to give her an extended tour of Europe. Although barred all over the southern United States from White restaurants and forced to sit in the back of buses and trains and use "colored only" facilities, in Europe Bethune was graciously received by the Pope in Rome, the Lord Mayor in London, and the Lord Provost in Edinburgh. Blessed with high self-esteem, uninhibited by her lowly beginnings, Mary McLeod Bethune was at home in any setting and proudly represented her gender, race, and profession wherever she went.

In the 1920s, she served as president of the National Association for Colored Women and the National Association of Teachers in Colored Schools. She was vice president of the National Association for the Advancement of Colored People (NAACP) and on the executive board of the National Urban League. She worked to obtain health care for minority children and facilities for delinquent Black girls separate from adult criminals, and fought against segregated public schools and the frequent lynchings of mostly Black males.

In 1938, President Franklin D. Roosevelt appointed Bethune as director of Negro Affairs in the National Youth Administration, the first U.S. post created for an African-American woman, where she strove for ten years to obtain jobs and college scholarships for minority youth. In 1937, she organized a highly successful National Conference on Problems of the Negro and Negro Youth, and invited Eleanor Roosevelt to give the opening address.

Realizing that Black women in America needed a clearinghouse for their isolated women's groups, Bethune created the National Council of Negro Women and, at age sixty, traveled across the country helping establish local clubs. Her goal was to improve housing, working conditions, living standards, educational and economic opportunities, and civil rights of minority citizens, especially women and children. In typical fashion, she bought a house for the Council in Washington, DC, with no means to pay for it, but certain that the money would be provided. Never shy about asking for help, she called on Marshall Field, III in Chicago, heir to the department store wealth, who was so impressed with her personality and work that he gave her a ten-thousand-dollar check for the house. The Council began a quarterly called *The Aframerican Woman's Journal* (later changed to *Women United*) and a monthly newsletter named *Telefact*. She also wrote columns for newspapers in Pittsburgh and Chicago.

Because Blacks in the 1940s were not allowed on the beautiful resort beaches in Florida, Bethune bought a large beach area for $200,000, incorporated the company and served as its president and treasurer for many years. Motels, a conference building, bathing and fishing facilities, and a dance hall were built exclusively for minority use. She also helped form the Central Life Insurance Company of Tampa so African Americans could buy homes via insurance. By 1952, she became its president—the only woman president of a life insurance company in America.

During World War II, Bethune was appointed assistant director of the Women's Army Auxiliary Corps (later known as WAC). She despised war as a way of solving conflicts, but once the United States was involved she worked hard recruiting Black women to serve in the armed services, getting Black nurses into army hospitals, and trying to break down segregation in the military. She was made an honorary general by the Women's Army for National Defense (WAND) and proudly wore a uniform with four stars on the shoulder.

In 1935, Bethune was awarded the Joel Spingarn gold medal by the NAACP "for the highest and noblest achievement for an American Negro." She was given the Drexel Award from Xavier University in New Orleans for "distinguished service to the betterment of humanity," and the Thomas Jefferson Award from the Southern Conference for Human Welfare for "outstanding service in the field of human welfare in line with the philosophy of Thomas Jefferson," the first African American to receive it. The Haitian government awarded her its highest honor, the Gold Medal of Honor, for her work in raising the esteem and bettering the lives of Blacks everywhere. Over the years, she also received eleven honorary college degrees—a great tribute to a child of slaves who was the first in her family to read and write.

Bethune was grief stricken at the sudden death of President Franklin D. Roosevelt and spoke at his memorial service, but to her delight, he bequeathed his walking stick to add to her collection of canes belonging to famous men. At the end of World War II, President Truman appointed her a consultant to the U.S. delegation at the United Nations Conference in San Francisco. In 1952, she was the official U.S. delegate to the inauguration of William Tubman, president of Liberia, and fulfilled a lifelong dream of touring Africa.

Despite chronic health problems, Bethune continued to speak and raise funds for moral causes, serve as an officer in various organizations, and accept honorary degrees. Rollins College in Winter Park, Florida, awarded her an honorary Doctor of Humanities degree—the first given to an African American from a White college in the south. Her last trip abroad was to the World Assembly for Moral Re-Armament in Caux, Switzerland, in 1954.

The following year, Mary McLeod Bethune died of a heart attack while staying at her beloved Bethune–Cookman Institute in Daytona. The college has established the Mary McLeod Bethune Foundation to house her papers and other archival material. In 1974, a bronze statue of her was erected in Lincoln Park in Washington, DC—the first on federal land in the nation's capitol to honor either a woman or an African American. In 1992, the Mary McLeod Bethune Council House, also in Washington DC, was designated a national historic site.

Mary McLeod Bethune's achievements have been an inspiration for young and old alike. Armed with her parents' love, a modest scholarship from a far-away White teacher, the support of dedicated teachers, and indomitable self-confidence and courage, she rose out of the cotton fields to become president of an accredited college and a national leader in the quest for rights and opportunities for African Americans. Undaunted by hardship and discrimination, sure of her own value as a human being, she refused to give "hate in return for hate" and thus won the friendship and affection of people of all races and social strata. In her "spiritual autobiography," she wrote, "Love, not hate has been the fountain of my fullness. In the streams of love that spring up within me, I have built my relationships with all mankind" (1948, 188).

Excerpts from Mary McLeod Bethune

In a 1940 interview with Dr. Charles S. Johnson, president of Fisk University in Nashville, Tennessee, Bethune revealed an incident in her childhood that had fueled her drive for education.

The first and real wound that I could feel in my soul and my mind was the realization of the dense darkness and ignorance that I found in myself. . . . I could see little white boys and girls going to school every day, learning to read and write; living in comfortable homes with all types of opportunities for growth and service. . . . I think that, actually, the first hurt that came to me in my childhood was the contrast of what was being done for the white children and lack of what we got. . . .

My mother kept in rather close contact with the people she served as a slave. She continued to cook for her master. . . . Very often I was taken along [to my mother's job] after I was old enough, and on one of these occasions . . . I went out into what they called their play house in the yard where they did their studying. They had pencils, slates, magazines and books. I picked up one of the books and one of the girls said to me—"You can't read that—put that down. I will show you some pictures over here," and when she said to me "You can't read that—put that down," it just did something to my pride and to my heart that made me feel that some day I would read just as she was reading. I did put it down, and followed her lead and looked at the picture book that she had. But I went away from there determined to learn how to read and that some day I would master for myself just what they were getting and it was that aim that I followed (1–2).

> To support herself and her students, most of whom could pay little if any tuition, Bethune wrote numerous letters to influential and wealthy people whom she hoped would see the value of her enterprise. Impressed by her intelligence, personality, goals, and perseverance, many donated generously over the years. However, without government or denominational aid, raising adequate funds remained a perennial and vexing problem. Next is Bethune's introductory letter to Booker T. Washington, the well-known founder of Tuskegee Institute, a school for African Americans in Alabama, who became her friend and supporter.

Letter to Booker T. Washington, November 3, 1902

Honored Sir:

I hope a note of this kind may not greatly surprise you, as a man in your sphere must expect such.

I am engaged in a Mission work in this town and I greatly desire your interest in it. It is an Interdenominational work therefore [it] has no support. It is a work that is most sadly needed to be done, and it takes great sacrifices to get it in shape. I have a rented room where I gather the poor and neglected children and teach them daily. Aside from this I do general city mission work, the jail work included. I have no support whatever save some few of the children who are able to pay a little tuition. Now I would like to ask you, would you recommend this humble work to some friend asking their assistance? Would you yourself make a donation toward helping us secure an organ for the Mission room? Do you know any friend who would even send a few [articles of] clothing to be used for the poor? God has wonderfully blessed you and used you and I know He will be pleased to have you lend your influence towards the sustenance of this work.

I trust you may consider well before answering.

Very respectfully,
Mary McLeod Bethune

> In her essay, *A Philosophy of Education for Negro Girls* (1926), Bethune outlined her reasons for establishing a school for African-American females and for promoting an education she felt suited their unique needs.

Early emancipation did not concern itself with giving advantages to Negro girls. The domestic realm was her field and no one sought to remove her. . . . Very early in my life, I saw the vision of what our women might contribute to the growth and development of the race—if they were given a certain type of intellectual training. I longed to see women, Negro women, hold in their hands diplomas which bespoke achievement; I longed to see them trained to be inspirational wives and mothers; I longed to see their accomplishments recognized side by side with any woman, anywhere. With this vision before me, my life has been spent. . . .

The education of the Negro girl must embrace a larger appreciation for good citizenship in the home. Our girls must be taught cleanliness, beauty and thoughtfulness and their application in making home life possible. For proper home life provides the proper atmosphere for life everywhere else. The ideals of home must not forever be talked about; they must be living factors built into the everyday educational experiences of our girls.

Negro girls must receive also a peculiar appreciation for the expression of the creative self. They must be taught to realize their responsibility [and] develop to the fullest extent the inner urges . . . that will lead them to be worthy contributors to the life of the little worlds in which they will live. This in itself will do more to remove the walls of inter-racial prejudice and build up intra-racial confidence and pride than many of our educational tools and devices (1–2).

> Bethune's "Sixth Annual Catalogue of the Daytona Educational and Industrial Training School for Negro Girls" (1910–1911) described her aim for the school and the rules that governed student behavior. Although the school was nondenominational, religious rituals and Bible study were an important part of daily life. However, said Bethune, "we seek guidance rather than creed."

The aim of this institution is to uplift Negro girls spiritually, morally, intellectually and industrially. The school stands for a broad, thorough practical training. To develop Christian character, to send forth women who will be rounded home-makers and Christian leaders is the aim of its founder and supporters, a trained mind, heart and hand being their idea of a complete education.

We try in governing our school to work by fundamental principles. We think education is as much for the sake of character as for knowledge. The purpose of order is to secure mental application and systemic development. We assume that our students want to know what is proper and right and we expect them to do it as fast as they know it, not because they have to, but because they want to. We teach them the moral law, the rules of propriety and good manners, and to give what is due in respect and obedience. No student is considered a model who either disobeys rules or has to be made to obey them. We are trying to get our students prepared for real life. We cannot and will not keep students who will not, at least, show a willingness to obey the rules and regulations. . . .

Students' correspondence is subject to inspection and regulations. Students must be vaccinated before entering school. Students and teachers are required to attend religious services in a body. Students are required to bring Bibles (2–3, 5).

> In 1923, Bethune's school for Black females was joined with a male institution to become Bethune–Cookman College, which is still in existence in Daytona, Florida. When the college became a fully accredited four-year institution, the curricular emphasis shifted more toward traditional academic subjects. Bethune, however, still believed strongly in the value of vocational training. In a letter to First Lady Eleanor Roosevelt (1941), who had agreed to serve on the Board of Trustees, Bethune expressed her desire to have more emphasis placed on "Vocational instruction in all of its phases." As always, music was a major part of her schools and a great personal joy.

If we are to build strong bodies we must begin to put emphasis on physical training. I would like to see here a fine class in Commercial dietetics, for this [is] a field where fine men and women may be developed with splendid cultural background. I am deeply interested in the secretarial courses, particularly those that prepare young women for service in personal care as well as in stenography, typewriting and filing. We need here in Bethune–Cookman a large gymnasium that may be used for recreation and for large gatherings of a musical or literary nature. We would then be in position to have artists like Marian Anderson and be prepared to take care of occasions such as we had when you came to us. There is nothing in this section where we may find participation in the cultural things save what we can provide ourselves.

I am determined to have our vocational work go forward on a parallel with our academic work. We look forward to four years of college work, preparing our young people as strongly in the vocations as in their literary pursuits. You know, of course, our need for a Library building and for more books. Our Library—inadequate though it is—is the only one for Negroes in Volusia County. We want to help our young people in Music—not only in training them in vocal, instrumental and choral music, but in publicizing and preserving their natural talents along this line. This is such a great field for development in so many phases of endeavor.

In an article in "The Southern Workman," Bethune (1934) described her beliefs concerning the value of a college education
and the major responsibilities of teachers: to be investigators,
interpreters, and inspirers.

Schools have two giant responsibilities: THE RESPONSIBILITY
OF INVESTIGATION and THE RESPONSIBILITY OF INTERPRE-
TATION. The man in the laboratory may investigate; the man in the
lecture room may interpret. But the teacher has a still diviner com-
mission than either the investigator or the interpreter. These men
deal with the matter of their subjects. The teacher must deal with
the minds of his students—minds that are plastic and can be shaped
into whatever the teacher's own character may design. Schools have
many functions, but their chief function is to furnish society with
three sorts of servants: investigators, interpreters, inspirers. . . . The
teacher's primary business is that of a stirrer-up. He is not, save sec-
ondarily, a salesman of knowledge. He is primarily, a stimulator of
knowledge and curiosity. But the good teacher manages to combine
all three functions to the ministry of his pupils. The good teacher
is an investigator. He is not content to squat behind the breast-
works of accumulated knowledge; he flirts with the unknown out
on the frontiers of knowledge; only so can he bring the spirit of
intellectual adventure and conquest into his classroom; an incuri-
ous teacher cannot stimulate curiosity.

The good teacher is also an INTERPRETER. He not only knows
more about his own subject than any other subjects but he knows
enough about other subjects to keep his subject in perspective. The
good teacher is an INSPIRER. He knows that the art of teaching lies
in starting something in the student's mind. He is not content with
merely putting something in the student's mind as a butcher stuffs
a sausage-skin. In short, therefore, the good teacher is an INVES-
TIGATOR, an INTERPRETER, an INSPIRER (200–202).

After the 1954 Supreme Court ruling in Brown v. Board of Education that required the desegregation of all public schools,
Bethune wrote in her column in the *Chicago Defender* (1955b)
why she believed this was needed.

INTEGRATION IS THE ONLY DEMOCRATIC WAY. The Supreme Court wisely saw this. The Justices knew when they rendered their decision that we stand at the crossroads in this issue. . . .

They considered the fact that the "separate but equal" theory was not real in practice: Negro schools have been separate but they have not been equal.

The Justices did not make their decision on this basis alone, however, for on this basis they could have declared educational facilities for Negroes inadequate and simply ordered better ones.

The basis on which the Court made its declaration was a great principle which is deep in the heart of democracy: SEGREGATION IS NOT DEMOCRATIC.

When the Court said that separate schools are IN PRINCIPLE unequal, they were not speaking merely of physical facilities. They were speaking of human principles. . . .

Social psychologists have spoken of the "split personality of our nation." Segregation is a sort of national Schizophrenia or split personality of the mind and the soul of America.

For the good of our own souls, segregation must go—from every quarter of our national life. . . .

In practicing racial discrimination we are not being democratic. And we cannot exist half-democratic. Integration of the races in public education is the only democratic way (10).

REFERENCES

Bethune, M. L. (1902). *Letter to Booker T. Washington*. Washington, DC: Booker T. Washington Papers, Library of Congress.

———. (1910–1911). *Sixth annual catalogue of the Daytona Educational and Industrial Training School for Negro Girls*. Tallahassee: Mary McLeod Bethune Papers, Florida State Archives.

———. (1926). *A philosophy of education for Negro girls*. New Orleans: Mary McLeod Bethune Papers, Amistad Research Center, Tulane University.

———. (1932). "The future college for the higher education of Negroes." In McKinney, T.E. (Ed.), *Higher education among Negroes* (59–65). Charlotte, NC: Johnson C. Smith University.

———. (1934, July). The educational values of the college-bred. *The Southern Workman*, 200–204.

———. (1940). *Charles S. Johnson interview*. Daytona Beach, FL: Mary McLeod Bethune Papers, Mary McLeod Bethune Foundation, Bethune–Cookman College.

———. (1941, April 22). *Letter to Eleanor Roosevelt*. Hyde Park, NY: Eleanor Roosevelt Papers, Franklin D. Roosevelt Library.

————. (1948). "Mary McLeod Bethune." In Finkelstein, L. (Ed.), *American spiritual autobiographies: Fifteen self-portraits* (182–190). New York: Harper & Brothers.

————. (1955a). "My Last Will and Testament." In McCluskey, A. T., & Smith, E. M. (Eds.) (1999). *Mary McLeod Bethune: Building a better world*. Bloomington: Indiana University Press.

————. (1955b, June 4). U.S. will make "the grade" in integrating all its schools. *Chicago Defender,* 10.

SELECTED OTHER WORKS BY
MARY MCLEOD BETHUNE

In F. J. Hicks (Ed.). (1975). *Mary McLeod Bethune: Her own words of inspiration*. Washington, DC: Nuclassics and Science.

Response, twenty-first Spingarn Medalist. (1935); Bethune-Cookman's next urgent step (1938); and numerous other short pieces. In McCluskey, A. T., & Smith, E. M. (Eds.), (1999). *Mary McLeod Bethune: Building a better world*. Bloomington: Indiana University Press.

SELECTED OTHER WORKS ABOUT
MARY MCLEOD BETHUNE

Hine, D. C., Brown, E. B., & Terborg-Penn, R. (Eds.). (1993). *Black women in America: An historical encyclopedia* (113–127). Brooklyn, NY: Carlson.

Holt, R. (1964). *Mary McLeod Bethune: A biography*. New York: Doubleday.

Peare, C. O. (1951). *Mary McLeod Bethune*. New York: Vanguard.

Rollins, C. H. (1964). *They showed the way: 40 American Negro leaders*. New York: Thomas Y. Crowell.

Smith, J. C. (Ed.). (1992). *Notable black women* (86–92). Detroit: Gale Research.

8

Helen Parkhurst:
Educating for Responsibility
with the Dalton Plan

Traditional schools in America in the 1920s were designed primarily to produce workers for industrial needs. Although a few young people would go to college and follow professional careers, most elementary and secondary students, especially in cities, entered the workforce as factory hands. What industrial managers wanted were employees who were punctual, obedient, and tolerant of long hours of tedious repetition and boredom. The school, with its captive audience, hierarchical organization, and clientele eager for future jobs, was exactly suited to model the factory and teach the desired behavior and values. What was not wanted in industry and most schools was independent thought, decision making, or creativity.

Among the few educators who fought this crippling of initiative and spirit was Helen Parkhurst, the creator of the Dalton Laboratory Plan. For a period in the 1920s and 1930s, this radical reorganization of schools was hailed as a panacea by progressive educators—an intellectual, exciting venture and humane way to manage the varied abilities and interests of students from fifth through twelfth grades. Dalton Plan schools lasted for the most part only a few decades in America, but they proliferated in other countries where they had a more enduring effect.

EARLY YEARS

Born in 1887 in Durand, Wisconsin, Helen Parkhurst grew up in a home filled with encouragement to explore, think, and create. At a time when many children's lives were regimented and rigid, this relaxed upbringing was unusual, especially for girls. Parkhurst credited a grandmother, in particular, for championing the right of children to choose and discover for themselves. Her brother, Alex Alden Parkhurst, also became a noted educator.

After graduating from high school at age fifteen, Parkhurst began her teaching career in a one-room rural school near her hometown. Here, her educational philosophy took rudimentary shape as she struggled to meet the needs of varied-age pupils with diverse abilities. In 1907, she graduated from Wisconsin State College in River Falls, having completed the usual four-year curriculum in two years, and two years later graduated from the distinguished Teachers College, Columbia University, New York City, where she studied with the famed philosopher John Dewey.

About this time, Parkhurst read Edgar James Swift's book, *Mind in the Making* (1908), which revolutionized her thought concerning what constitutes education and how students learn. From that book rose her ideas for organizing classrooms into "educational laboratories" where teachers work alongside students, rather than dominate them, and where students have ample time to do thorough work on their studies instead of being hustled by bell from class to class and subject to subject. This constant interruption, said Parkhurst, results in students who fail to appreciate the importance of work—a failure frequently noted by teachers of all periods in the history of education.

TEACHING EXPERIENCE

In 1910, Parkhurst moved to Tacoma, Washington, where she quickly became noted for her innovative educational views and success with children. She convinced the Board of Education to let her use the laboratory plan in her classes and soon was made First Citizen of Tacoma, given a Gold Medal, and a one thousand dollar award—an amazing recognition for a twenty-four-year-old woman in her first years of teaching, especially when advocating an approach radically different from prevailing practices.

In 1913, she returned to Wisconsin to join the faculty at Central State Teachers' College (now the University of Wisconsin–Stevens Point). The following year, she traveled to Italy to study anthropology at the University of Rome. While there, she visited a slum area where a young woman doctor, Maria Montessori, was having remarkable success teaching sixty poor, preschool children to read and write. Impressed, Parkhurst enrolled in the Montessori Training School and later lived with the famous educator for several years.

After three years at Stevens Point, Parkhurst moved east where she hoped to find greater acceptance for her ideas. Appointed head of the Children's Education Foundation in New York City, she established the Children's University School to further develop her laboratory method. She was also chosen by Montessori to head the Montessori Training Department in New York City, the first and for a long time the only person the Italian doctor authorized to train her teachers in the United States.

In 1916, Parkhurst was invited by a boys' school, the Upway School for Crippled Children in Pittsfield, Massachusetts, to design an ungraded, individualized program for students. A year later, she implemented an expanded version in a public high school for boys and girls in the nearby town of Dalton—hence the name, the Dalton Plan. She wanted to honor the teachers and the school system where her educational ideas were first fully developed.

Although Maria Montessori had also instituted a scheme for secondary pupils, following the success of her elementary program, her stress was on practical, daily living skills for rural youth. Parkhurst's design was an academic curriculum for those in urban schools and resembled Montessori's only in its emphasis on student freedom and self-discipline.

For two decades, Parkhurst helped establish Dalton Laboratory Plan schools, not only across America, but in other countries where they were more widely received and longer lasting. The Children's University School in New York City, instituted in 1919 and later renamed The Dalton School, is still thriving today. In its current version, the school makes good use of advanced technology, a highly educated faculty, and wonderful community resources, such as the many museums. Helen Parkhurst remained head mistress until 1942 when at age fifty-five she resigned to become a First Fellow in Education at Yale University.

AIMS AND PRINCIPLES OF THE DALTON PLAN

Like the progressive philosopher John Dewey, Helen Parkhurst was interested in all aspects of a child's development—social and physical as well as intellectual. She emphasized the importance of living in the present, rather than studying abstract and fragmented subjects on the chance that they might some day be useful to some children. Under the Dalton Plan, therefore, students were given opportunities to experience social living and democratic freedoms, and all studies were designed to have a clear relevance either to the present or a foreseeable future. Facts were not learned in isolation, but seen as parts of a whole and integrated with other disciplines.

Dalton Plan teachers believed that children are eager to learn if the material and activities are interesting and perceived to be of value to them. The focus was always on the learner. Curriculum planners studied the pupils to discover what they were capable of doing, what interested them, what motivated them to work diligently, what they found difficult, and what they retained over a long period. "The true business of school," said Parkhurst, "is not to chain the pupil to preconceived ideas, but to set him free to discover his own ideas and help him to bring all his power to bear upon the problem of learning" (1922, 151–152). Educators, she maintained, often confuse instruction and learning. Traditional classrooms revolve around the teacher, who daily decides for students the subject content, the activities, and the amount of time and effort required. Many teachers know their subject well and work hard presenting it, but one person cannot force another to learn. Since students vary widely in their interests and abilities, only a few at any one time are fully tuned into a teacher's planned program and learn what is expected.

In contrast to traditional methods, the Dalton system had three major emphases: (a) freedom to choose each day the subject, level, quantity, and pace; (b) contracts in each subject that encouraged independent thinking, risk-taking, and creativity as well as acquisition of knowledge; and (c) teacher and peer availability for help. The aim was to produce students who were industrious, responsible, open-minded, and eager to gain and apply knowledge. An essential element was trust. Teachers had to believe that students could control themselves if given freedom to make decisions, and students had to believe that their teacher's main goal was to help them succeed to the best of their ability.

Traditional schools, noted Parkhurst, barely tap the surface of children's energies and aptitudes. She wished to go deeper, to unleash powers by letting pupils ascertain their own difficulties and find ways to overcome them. This freedom to choose, however, did not mean license. Individuals who do whatever they want are not free, she noted, but are chained to eventual consequences. In a Dalton Plan school, students could make choices within a richly planned environment, but were not allowed to run wild, infringe on the rights of others, or throw away their chance for an education.

THE DALTON METHOD

Instituting the Dalton Laboratory Plan required a complete school reorganization. Typically, the day was divided into academic and nonacademic subjects, with the first studied in the mornings in an individualized approach and the latter taught by large group methods in the afternoons. The curriculum for each grade and subject was divided into units, one for each month. Each unit was then broken into subunits with the goals for each clearly spelled out so students could see the whole, but be able to handle it in smaller, manageable pieces. At the beginning of the month, students were given a contract in each subject area, with activities included for differing ability levels and learning strategies.

Each contract was built around a central idea and contained a variety of useful and interesting activities to aid in understanding the topic and applying new knowledge. Students were required to do the first level to ensure an understanding of basic concepts and information, but could then choose how much more they wanted to do and at what level of difficulty. Their grade was determined by objective test scores as well as the quality and quantity of the contract work, with quality and originality given highest rank. Students were rewarded for experimentation and creativity. The contracts were not programmed learning packets with right and wrong answers, but open-ended inquiries calling for judgment, risk-taking, and independent thought.

The central feature of this organizational plan was the laboratory. A room (or several if the school were large) was set up for each subject and all the work was done in the respective lab. At least one specialist teacher was available in each room for consultation. Tables and chairs replaced desks so pupils could work individually, in pairs, or in small groups. All books and materials related to the subject were moved from the library and stockroom to the subject labs, and contract projects required frequent use of sophisticated resource materials.

All students were assigned to a "house," a classroom where they met each morning for a conference with a homeroom teacher/ advisor to determine the day's plan. From there, students could go to any lab that was not crowded and work on any part of their contract for that subject for as long as desired. There were no bells, schedules, or mass movement between classes. They could move around at will within a lab, cooperate with other students or work alone, and seek help from their peers or the specialists. Subject lab teachers made no assignments beyond the contracts, gave no lectures, and made no large-group announcements—although they worked with individuals or small groups of students who were having similar difficulties or wanted to discuss a topic. In the afternoons, students attended traditional large group classes such as music and physical education and participated in extracurricular activities of their choice.

Only a few regulations guided the students' behavior:

1. Once a laboratory was selected, students had to remain there for at least an hour to ensure that sufficient work was done on a contract. They could not flit from room to room. However, at the end of the hour they could move to another lab or stay as long as they wished. Those students who did well in all subjects were urged not to spend more than two hours in any one lab, whereas those who had difficulty in a particular subject were encouraged to remain and request help. However, if a student had a special interest or talent in one subject and was moving ahead on all contracts, he or she was permitted to spend as much time as desired in the preferred lab.

2. Students were not to disturb the concentration of others or take materials away from someone using them. Talking quietly about contract activity was permitted and small discussion groups could be formed, but both students and teachers had to respect the right of others at all times to work in uninterrupted peace.

3. Students had to use materials carefully and appropriately and return them to their proper places. Labs were sufficiently stocked and contracts varied so that most of the time students could quickly obtain what they needed. When labs grew crowded, preference was given to those students who needed to finish a particular contract or were having problems. Others were urged to choose another lab and return at a later time.

4. Students had to satisfactorily complete a contract in each subject area for a given period (usually a month) before they received a new set. This prevented them from avoiding those subjects they disliked or had difficulty with and spending all their time on those they favored. If all contracts were finished early, students could request the next set or return to labs of choice for more practice or for activities of their own design until the next month began. Most preferred to move ahead with a new set.

Assignment Contracts

The success of the Dalton Plan hinged not only on the students' freedom to choose but the quality of the assignments. In her book, *Education on the Dalton Plan* (1922), Parkhurst included a number of contract samples for upper elementary students to illustrate the types of activities she believed most educational and engaging. For instance, students were often asked to read a selection and discuss the significance of certain aspects. In science they might be told to gather specimens, examine them, draw them, and classify them. In social studies they might be directed to collect data from contemporary sources about a particular social problem and suggest alternative ways of solving it.

Contracts were written so that students of differing ability levels could achieve success, not just the brighter ones. Students could read the instructions as often as necessary and proceed on their own or with a partner or small group. Each aspect of the assignment was simply and clearly expressed, in a conversational tone, and explained how the work would help achieve a goal. Hints were given on where information could be found or how difficult parts could be tackled. Although students could work with others and ask for help, the activities were designed not to surpass an individual's ability, so accomplishment could be achieved alone.

A typical contract contained three groups of activities: one that was essential to understand the topic, which everyone was required to do; another that called for more thinking and effort; and a third that challenged the most talented. After doing the first group, students could choose from the others and stop when they wished. Because their grades depended on the amount and quality achieved on their contracts, students were motivated to try more difficult tasks, but were not compelled to go beyond their abilities to reach their monthly goal. For those few students at either extreme—who found the lowest level too difficult or the highest too easy—contracts were adjusted by the laboratory specialist to meet their particular needs. Most of the students easily discovered their level within the assigned contract and worked to that end.

Although contracts were designed to be done completely in the labs, students could take them home if they chose. They could work ahead, catch up on days missed by illness or other absences, or have more time to do activities in the labs they most enjoyed. However, there was no homework requirement or penalty for not doing work outside of school. If students worked hard all day, it was felt, they should use their evening hours to pursue interests such as music and sports, read for pleasure, or just relax (as most adults do after a day's work).

Because students worked at their own speed and chose their own level, some finished long before others. A bright, ambitious child could complete thirteen or more contracts in a ten-month school year, whereas another, because of slowness, illness, or excessive absences, might finish only seven or eight. This posed no problem for the school, however, for the quicker child was simply promoted when the ten contracts were completed (at any time during the year) and began the next grade's set. Students who finished all high school contracts ahead of time could graduate early and enter college or the workforce if desired. Or they could stay in high school to participate in extracurricular activities and do more advanced contracts in chosen labs or design their own projects.

The children who had academic difficulties were not pushed beyond their abilities, but given as much time and help as needed to understand and complete their work. Although they progressed more slowly, and worked at a simplified level, they mastered far more than in traditional classrooms where their teachers and peers necessarily had to move on to newer or more challenging tasks. In Dalton Plan schools students picked up at the beginning of each school year where they left off in the spring and were promoted to a new grade level any time during the year when all ten contracts were satisfactorily completed. The only consequence for those who did not finish all ten during the year was that another six months or year might be needed to complete them. The benefits were that no one graduated who had not mastered at least the basics of each subject and the extra time produced a more confident and competent adult.

Most Dalton Plan schools retained the standard ten-month school year, but Parkhurst believed a twelve-month schedule was more beneficial to students because the long summer break caused forgetfulness and created lassitude. Because work was done independently, vacations could be taken at any time during the year without concern for what was missed in the classrooms. As long as contracts were written up in advance, teachers also could select vacation times on an individual basis since substitutes could easily handle the subject labs when students took responsibility for their daily work.

Evaluation Techniques

In order to keep detailed records of what children were accomplishing, Parkhurst created a system of graphs—one for each laboratory teacher, one for each student, and one for the home advisor. The laboratory graph that resided on the bulletin board listed all the students' names in each homeroom. Before leaving a lab, pupils marked on this graph the amount of work done that period. The lab teacher and students could see at a glance the progress being made (or not made) by each individual. This graph was a good motivator when procrastinators fell behind their peers. It did not indicate the difficulty of the contract or quality of the work done, which would embarrass the students, but merely how much of a contract was accomplished each day in that particular lab. It also showed the instructor which individuals were probably in need of help. If a pupil was putting forth effort but having major trouble doing a contract, the work was made easier until the individual could achieve success. The next contract was then adjusted accordingly so that the student could move ahead on his or her own, no matter what the level.

The pupils' individualized graphs recorded the progress in all subjects, so they could readily see which contracts were nearing completion and which needed more work. This was an excellent aid in time-management, keeping students from spending too much time on any one subject and neglecting others. The house advisor's graph listed all pupils' names and recorded their progress each week in all subjects. Again, students could compare their progress with peers and help each other complete work, and the advisor could discover why certain students were falling behind and offer support.

No contracts were evaluated for quality until finished, although a daily check for progress was made by means of the graphs. When completed, a contract was graded by the lab specialist—but holistically, not each separate part, which gave a better picture of the students' overall understanding and cut down on the time spent grading. Before turning in a contract, students could revise as often as they wanted until satisfied it was the best they could do. They could also seek help from the teacher or their peers. Any contract that was not judged satisfactory was returned for more effort, so no advantage was found in doing hurried or sloppy work.

The other measure of evaluation used in Dalton Plan schools was objective tests, which students took individually when ready. If mastery of basic material was not demonstrated, students returned to a lab for additional work before obtaining a new set of contracts. However, by working diligently in the lab or at home, students who fell behind could catch up if they chose. Because contracts were designed so that even those with low abilities could succeed at some level, the usual reason for not completing lab work or passing a test was lack of effort. Thus, in Dalton Plan schools, the responsibility for learning was placed squarely on the shoulders of each student, and no one was passed along until mastery was evident.

ROLE OF THE TEACHER

Like teachers in Montessori schools, those who worked under the Dalton Plan assumed a different role from traditional instructors. Besides being knowledgeable in their field of specialization, they needed to understand child and adolescent psychology in order to incorporate activities appropriate for the age and maturity level of their students. They also needed to be patient, courteous, congenial, and calm. Instead of demanding attention and obedience, they became facilitators, counselors, older friends to whom the students looked for guidance and support. Their mission was to help students develop their talents and strengths, improve their weaknesses, and progress in their knowledge of particular subject matter.

The most difficult part was gearing the contracts to the differing levels so students were not working above their ability, nor beneath it. The contracts had to be challenging but achievable, interesting and informative, varied in their activities, and interrelated as much as possible with other subjects. Obviously this required skill, knowledge, time, and dedication on the part of teachers. Working under the Dalton Laboratory Plan was definitely not easy. However, teachers reported greater satisfaction than they had experienced in traditional schools, for they liked being friends and helpers to students rather than disciplinarians. They also enjoyed the opportunity for greater collegiality with fellow teachers and felt less isolation. Afternoons were used by subject lab instructors to work together in small groups sharing ideas, solving problems, writing contracts, and evaluating student work. Teaching became a shared activity and the workload was more evenly distributed.

BENEFITS OF THE DALTON PLAN

For Students

The major benefit was the effect on students. Working alone or in groups of their choice, they learned to be independent thinkers, to trust their judgments, to experiment with new ideas and methods, and to see temporary failure as a learning device rather than a personality defect. Having the time to work at length on something that either interested them or was causing difficulty brought achievement and strengthened natural talents. Pupils were neither held back by others nor pushed to do more complicated matters when they did not understand what went before. All students worked at their own pace and received help from the teacher-specialist or peers as needed. At the same time, they learned that, as in life, some work needs to be done whether one wants to do it or not. Although they may have disliked or had trouble with certain subjects, all contracts had to be completed before they could move ahead in any area, which taught self-discipline and fortitude.

A second benefit was the development of cooperation and caring. Those who learned quickly were often moved by compassion and friendship to help their slower companions. They voluntarily gave suggestions on how to complete a project and where to find information, or explained a concept in adolescent terminology that was more meaningful to a fellow student than the written materials or the teacher's words. Unlike today's emphasis on "cooperative learning," however, no one was forced into particular groups and required to help others, nor were their grades tied to the work habits or abilities of group-mates. Students were encouraged to both give and receive aid, but were permitted to work alone if they preferred. Most students in the Dalton Plan did some of each.

Because this plan encouraged informality and helpfulness, withdrawn students gained self-confidence through interaction with their peers and the laboratory teacher. Shy children who were frightened of talking before a large group participated willingly in small group discussions, and individual conferences with a friendly teacher developed the ability to talk with an adult and express ideas and concerns in an articulate manner. Furthermore, the slower children were not separated from their brighter companions. Students of varying ages and abilities worked in the labs at the same time, but at self-chosen paces on different projects. None were labeled "college-bound" or "remedial," and those who made the most gains in this plan were the ones previously showing little interest or progress.

Another benefit was that new students were easily accommodated. Children who entered a Dalton school in the middle of the year posed no problem even if they were behind or ahead in certain subjects. By means of diagnostic tests, each lab instructor determined what the child knew about the subject and assigned a contract accordingly, adjusting as needed. Students were encouraged to offer friendship and to help the new person become comfortable with the system. Those who were ill for a length of time also benefited. Contracts could be completed at home or hospital if the children were able. When they returned to school, they picked up where they left off without missing crucial material or instructions as in traditional classrooms. In such cases, contracts were often shortened, with fewer enrichment activities, so the child could catch up faster.

Absences of any kind—for vacation, funerals, family crises—were handled in a similar manner. Students unable to complete a month's work simply continued on contracts until they were finished, getting a new set when ready. Thus, a few students, whether from absences, mental disabilities, or personal problems, needed more than ten months to complete all contracts, whereas others finished early and moved on to the next year's work. A student who fell behind for whatever reason was penalized only in the sense that more time was needed before promotion, which could take place any time during the school year.

For Teachers and the School District

The major benefits for teachers were being able to specialize, spend all their time on teaching activities, develop friendly relations with students, create interesting and challenging contracts, work without arbitrary schedules, have time to help those in need, and cooperate with colleagues. They felt less stress and a greater sense of achievement in their chosen career.

Because classes in secondary schools were neither age- nor ability-grouped and all labs were open to all students, scheduling problems were eliminated. The costs of adopting the Dalton Plan were limited, as existing rooms were utilized without major remodeling and faculty were assigned according to their specialties. Because the students were at all times actively involved in learning activities and more highly motivated to complete their work, far fewer discipline problems occurred. Furthermore, all students who graduated from a Dalton Plan school could clearly demonstrate at least a basic competence in all subject areas.

In short, the Dalton Laboratory Plan, according to its supporters, produced graduates who were masters of themselves as well as their environment; motivated workers who were creative and independent; and cooperative, caring individuals who knew how to live in social harmony.

THE CRITICS: DIFFICULTIES WITH THE DALTON PLAN

As with any radical change, time and patience was needed to reorganize a school along the laboratory plan—perhaps even more than usual. Students who had been trained for years to be dependent on teachers and schedules did not overnight become independent workers and thinkers. They needed help in changing their work habits, expectations, and attitudes. Parkhurst reported, however, that a conversion was usually made within a few months if the teaching staff was solidly behind the program. Once trust was developed, and students realized they did indeed have freedom to make choices, to talk quietly, to get help when needed, to move from lab to lab at will, they became absorbed in their work, proud of their accomplishments, and eager to move ahead.

Teachers, too, needed time to adjust. Accustomed to large group teaching and conformity, many were initially fearful of putting so much control in the hands of students. The Dalton Plan required a belief that children want to learn, are capable of doing much on their own, and will work earnestly and be self-disciplined when a task has a clear purpose and is interesting and attainable. Teachers who did not believe these things, who did not trust young people, and who could not relax and be friendly guides, found the Dalton Plan intolerable. Such persons in a Dalton Plan school could undermine the success of this program. However, said Parkhurst, often those who were at first doubtful or even hostile to the laboratory arrangement later became its strongest supporters when they experienced firsthand the benefits and saw how superior it was to the traditional classroom method.

The biggest problem for teachers was the time, effort, expertise, and creativity necessary to design appropriate contracts, as well as an in-depth knowledge of each student's abilities and difficulties. Although the graph method of keeping track of pupil progress in each subject was helpful, this too became cumbersome over time. The technology available in the twenty-first century would greatly facilitate the record-keeping needed for a Dalton Plan school to function efficiently.

LATER YEARS AND LASTING ACHIEVEMENTS

The Dalton Laboratory Plan received much publicity in America during the 1920s and 1930s, but had a greater and more lasting impact in foreign countries. Parkhurst's first invitation was from England in 1921 to give a series of lectures, and soon after the Dalton Association was organized there. In 1922, the New York publishing house, E. P. Dutton, produced her book *Education on the Dalton Plan*, which explained the laboratory method in detail. In 1928, she was asked to establish Dalton Plan schools in Chile and in subsequent years was invited to Denmark, Germany, The Netherlands, China, India, France, Japan, and the Soviet Union. When she was a delegate to a world education conference in Africa in 1934, Parkhurst's speaking skills and ideas won acclaim when she stepped in as the opening keynote speaker for John Dewey, who had become ill.

In 1925, the first president of the Chinese Republic decorated Parkhurst with the Order of Merit for her contribution to Chinese education. In Japan, where the Dalton Plan was especially well-received, she was decorated by the emperor for her influence on Japanese schools. In 1952, the "Helen Parkhurst Dalton School" was dedicated in Rotterdam—the only school in Denmark until that time to be named for an American. Five years later, Parkhurst was decorated by Queen Juliana of The Netherlands for her innovative ideas established there. Although she declined an invitation to the Soviet Union because of commitments to Japan, Parkhurst's book on the Dalton Plan was translated into Russian by the wife of the revolutionary Vladimer Lenin. Within the next ten years, fifteen books on the laboratory method were written by Soviet educators.

From 1947 to 1954, Helen Parkhurst became a radio and television personality, popular with children, parents, and educators. Her first program was "Child's World" for the American Broadcasting Company. On "One World" and "Growing Pains," she interviewed children and teenagers, without judgment, on their views and experiences on such topics as anger and prejudice. She was also a regular panelist on a weekly television show called "The World of Sound." Many of Parkhurst's programs were made into records, which sold widely in the United States and other countries.

Helen Parkhurst died in New Milford, Connecticut, in 1973. Some of the above records, along with newspaper clippings and other memorabilia, can be found in the archives at the University of Wisconsin-Stevens Point, where she taught for three years. The year after her death, the university dedicated a lecture hall in her memory. Before she died, Parkhurst was working on two books, one about Maria Montessori and the other on her own happy childhood in Wisconsin. From both these influences came her belief that when children are trusted, given freedom to explore within well-thought boundaries, and are allowed to choose their interests and move at their own pace, they will become disciplined, eager, lifelong learners as well as self-assured, socially mature individuals.

Excerpts from Helen Parkhurst

In the 1920s and 1930s, Helen Parkhurst's method of individualized learning was an innovative and controversial approach.
Her book, *Education on the Dalton Plan* (1922), described in
detail how teachers taught responsibility by giving students
freedom to control their time and studies. Schools that fully
adopted the plan, both in America and other countries, reported great success in academic achievement as well as in self-
discipline, cooperation, and independent thinking. Parkhurst
was highly critical of the teacher-centered, bell-driven, and one-
size-fits-all curriculum that was common in most schools, both
public and private.

[School should be] a sociological laboratory where the pupils
themselves are the experimenters, not the victims of an intricate and
crystallized system in whose evolution they have neither part nor
lot. Let us think of it as a place where community conditions prevail as they prevail in life itself. . . . [The goal of the Dalton Plan is]
to revitalize education—to make it a living thing capable of arous-
ing and preserving the interest of pupils in their work (16–17).

Broadly speaking the old type of school may be said to stand for
culture, while the modern type of school stands for *experience.* The
Dalton Laboratory Plan is primarily a way whereby both these aims
can be reconciled and achieved.

The acquisition of culture is a form of experience, and as such is
an element in the business of living with which school ought to be
as intimately concerned as is adult existence. But it will never become so until the school as a whole is reorganized so that it can
function like a community—a community whose essential condition is freedom for the individual to develop himself.

This ideal freedom is not license, still less indiscipline. It is, in
fact, the very reverse of both. The child who "does as he likes" is
not a free child. He is, on the contrary, apt to become the slave of
bad habits, selfish and quite unfit for community life. Under these
circumstances he needs some means of liberating his energy before
he can grow into a harmonious, responsible being, able and willing to lend himself consciously to cooperation with his fellows for
their common benefit. The Dalton Laboratory Plan provides that
means by diverting his energy to the pursuit and organization of
his own studies in his own way. It gives him that mental and moral
liberty which we recognize as so necessary on the physical plane

in order to insure his bodily well-being. Anti-social qualities and activities are, after all, merely misdirected energy.

Freedom is therefore the first principle of the Dalton Laboratory Plan. From the academic, or cultured, point of view, the pupil must be made free to continue his work upon any subject in which he is absorbed without interruption, because when interested he is mentally keener, more alert, and more capable of mastering any difficulty that may arise in the course of his study. Under the new method there are no bells to tear him away at an appointed hour and chain him pedagogically to another subject and another teacher. Thus treated, the energy of the pupil automatically runs to waste. Such arbitrary transfers are indeed as uneconomic as if we were to turn an electric stove on and off at stated intervals for no reason. Unless a pupil is permitted to absorb knowledge at his own rate of speed he will never learn anything thoroughly. Freedom is taking his own time. To take someone else's time is slavery (18–19).

> Although a major aim was to promote students' independent thinking and self-reliance, another goal was the formation of community, where they developed social skills, became interdependent and cooperative, respected various viewpoints, and unselfishly helped each other to succeed.

The second principle of the Dalton Laboratory Plan is cooperation or, as I prefer to call it, the interaction of group life. . . . Under the old educational system a pupil can and often does live outside his group, touching it only when he passes in company with his fellows over the common mental highway called the curriculum. This easily ends in his becoming anti-social, and if so he carries this handicap with him when he leaves school for the wider domain of life. Such a pupil may even be an "intelligent participator" in the life of his form or class, just as a teacher may be. But a democratic institution demands more than this. Real social living is more than contact; it is cooperation and interaction. A school cannot reflect the social experience which is the fruit of community of life unless all its parts, or groups, develop those intimate relations one with the other and that interdependence which, outside school, binds men and nations together (19–20).

> The primary aim of a Dalton Laboratory school was for students to develop responsibility and self-discipline and a love

for learning by giving them freedom of choice and authentic tasks.

[School] should be so organized that neither pupil nor teacher can isolate themselves, nor escape their due share in the activities and in the difficulties of others. We all know the teachers who hang up their personality each morning as they hang up their coats. Outside school these people have human interests and human charm which they do not dare to exhibit when with their pupils lest they should in so doing seem to abrogate their authority. The Dalton Laboratory Plan has no use for the parade of such fictitious authority, which is restrictive, not educative. Instead of promoting order it provokes indiscipline. It is fatal to the idea of a school as a vital social unit.

Equally, from the pupil's point of view, is the child when submitted to the action of arbitrary authority and to immutable rules and regulations, incapable of developing a social consciousness which is the prelude to that social experience so indispensable as a preparation for manhood and womanhood. Academically considered, the old system is just as fatal as it is from the social point of view. A child never voluntarily undertakes anything that he does not understand. The choice of his games or pursuits is determined by a clear estimate of his capabilities to excel in them. Having the responsibility of his choice his mind acts like a powerful microscope, taking in and weighing every aspect of the problem he must master in order to ensure success. Given the same free conditions his mind would act on the problems of study in exactly the same way. Under the Dalton Laboratory Plan we place the work problem squarely before him, indicating the standard which has to be attained. After that he is allowed to tackle it as he thinks fit in his own way and at his own speed. Responsibility for the result will develop not only his latent intellectual powers, but also his judgment and character (21–22). . . .

Briefly summarized, the aim of the Dalton Plan is a synthetic aim. It suggests a simple and economic way by means of which the school as a whole can function as a community. The conditions under which the pupils live and work are the chief factors of their environment, and a favorable environment is one which provides opportunities for spiritual as well as mental growth. It is the social experience accompanying the tasks, not the tasks themselves, which stimulates and furthers both these kinds of growth. Thus the Dalton Plan lays emphasis upon the importance of the child's living while he does his work, and the manner in which he acts as a member of society, rather than upon the subjects of his curriculum. It is the sum total of these twin experiences which determines his character and his knowledge (29–30).

> Students were aided in this self-education and decision making by viewing the twelve-month contracts at the beginning of the school year, or whenever they were ready for the next grade. They could see what was expected in each subject area, estimate what they would probably be able to accomplish and at what level of difficulty, and budget their time accordingly. They could, of course, alter their plans along the way, but an initial perusal of the year's work gave them a sense of direction and resulted in satisfaction and pride as each set of contracts was completed.

In order that [a student] may be led to educate himself—we must give him an opportunity to survey the whole of the task we set. To win the race he must first get a clear view of the goal. It would be well to lay a whole twelve month's work before the pupil at the beginning of the school year. This will give him a perspective of the plan of his education. He will thus be able to judge of the steps he must take each month and each week so that he may cover the whole road, instead of going blindly forward with no idea either of the road or the goal. How so handicapped can a child be expected to be interested in the race even to desire to win it? How can a teacher hope to turn out a well-equipped human being unless he takes the trouble to study the psychology of the child? Both for master and for pupil a perception of their job is essential. Education is, after all, a cooperative task. Their success or failure in it is interlocked.

Children learn, if we would only believe it, just as men and women learn, by adjusting means to ends. What does a pupil do when given, as he is given by the Dalton Laboratory Plan, responsibility for the performance of such and such work? Instinctively he seeks the best way of achieving it. Then having decided, he proceeds to act upon that decision. Supposing his plan does not seem to fit his purpose, he discards it and tries another. Later on he may find it profitable to consult his fellow students engaged in a similar task. Discussion helps to clarify his ideas and also his plan of procedure. When he comes to the end the finished achievement takes on all the splendor of success. It embodies all he has thought and felt and lived during the time it has taken to complete. This is real experience. It is culture acquired through individual development and through collective cooperation. It is no longer school—it is life.

Not only will this method of education stimulate the deepest interest and the highest powers in a student, but it will teach him how to proportion effort to attainment . . . the child's attack upon his problem of work should be facilitated by allowing him to concentrate all his forces upon the subject that claims his interest at one particular moment. He will in this case not only do more work, but better work too. The Dalton Laboratory Plan permits pupils to budget their time and to spend it according to their need (22–24).

> The curriculum, Parkhurst stressed, is a means to an end, not the end itself. It serves a larger purpose: that of teaching students how to learn, to discover what they find of most interest, and to acquire sufficient knowledge to aid them in living in social communities. Thus, a curriculum should never be set in stone, but should fluctuate depending on students' needs and the best judgments of the teachers.

But as liberty is an integral part of that ideal I have carefully guarded against the temptation to make my plan a stereotyped cast-iron thing ready to fit any school anywhere. So long as the principle that animates it is preserved, it can be modified in practice in accordance with the circumstances of the school and the judgment of the staff. For this reason I refrain from dogmatizing on what subjects should be included in the curriculum, or by what standards the achievement of pupils should be measured. Above all, I do not want to canalize the life-blood of citizenship. On this point I can but say that the curriculum of any school should vary according to the needs of the pupils, and even in schools where it is designed to serve a definite academic purpose, this aspect should not be lost sight of as it often is. Until the educational world wakes to the fact that curriculum is not the chief problem of society, we shall, I fear, continue to handicap our youth by viewing it through the wrong end of the telescope.

Today we think too much of curricula and too little about the boys and girls. The Dalton Plan is not a panacea for academic ailments. It is a plan through which the teacher can get at the problem of child psychology and the pupil at the problem of learning.

It diagnoses school situations in terms of boys and girls. Subject difficulties concern students, not teachers. The curriculum is but our technique, a means to an end. The instrument to be played upon is the boy or girl.

Under the conditions that exist in the average school the energies of these boys and girls cannot flow freely. The top-heavy organization has been built up for the instructor, and with it teachers are expected to solve their problems. But I contend that the real problem of education is not a teacher's but a pupil's problem. All the difficulties that harass the teacher are created by the unsolved difficulties of the pupils. When the latter disappear the former will vanish also, but not before the school organization and its attendant machinery has been re-made for the pupil, who is rendered inefficient and irritable by being compelled to use a mechanism that is not his own.

The first thing, therefore, is to remove all impediments that prevent the pupil from getting at his problem. Only he knows what his real difficulties are, and unless he becomes skilled in dispersing them he will become skilled in concealing them. Hitherto our educational system has been content to tap the surface water of his energy. Now we must try to reach and release the deep well of his natural powers. In doing so we shall assist and encourage the expression of his life-force and harness it to the work of education. This is not to be achieved by doing the pupil's work for him, but by making it possible for him to do his own work. Harmony between teacher and pupil is essential if we would avoid those emotional conflicts which are the most distracting among the ills the old type of school is heir to.

Experience of the Dalton Laboratory Plan shows, moreover, that it is beneficial to the pupils morally as well as mentally. Where it is put into operation conflicts cease, disorder disappears. The resistance generated in the child by the old inelastic machinery to the process of learning is transformed into acquiescence, and then into interest and industry as soon as he is released to carry out the educational program in his own way. Freedom and responsibility together perform the miracle (27–29).

REFERENCES

Parkhurst, H. (1922). *Education on the Dalton Plan.* New York: E. P. Dutton. (Published in 58 languages)

Swift, E. J. (1908). *Mind in the making: A study in mental development*. New York: Scribner's.

SELECTED OTHER WORKS BY HELEN PARKHURST

Exploring the Child's World (1951). New York: Appleton, Century, Crofts. Introduction by Aldous Huxley. Printed in six languages and chosen by the U.S. government to go behind the Iron Curtain in German language translation.
Growing Pains (1962). New York: Doubleday. Introduction by William Heard Kilpatrick. A book about teenagers.
Recordings of Parkhurst's broadcast interviews, "Child's World," "One World," and "Growing Pains," are available at the University of Wisconsin-Stevens Point archives.
Parkhurst also wrote many articles for education journals and art magazines.

SELECTED OTHER WORKS ABOUT HELEN PARKHURST

Birch, A. W. (1973, March/April). *The perennial Helen Parkhurst*. In archives, University of Wisconsin-Stevens Point.
Blois, B. (no date) *The development and implementation of Helen Parkhurst's Dalton Plan*. Unpublished paper. In archives, University of Wisconsin-Stevens Point.

SELECTED WORKS ABOUT THE DALTON LABORATORY PLAN

The Education Index covering 1929–1938 lists nearly fifty articles lauding the Dalton Plan.
Bassett, R. (1922). *Dalton Plan assignments* (Vol. 1 & 2). London: G. Bell & Sons.
Dewey, E. (1922). *The Dalton Laboratory Plan*. New York: Dutton.
Lynch, A. J. (1925). *Individual work and the Dalton Plan*. London: George Philip & Son.
Members of the Faculty of the South Philadelphia High School for Girls. (1927). *Educating for responsibility: The Dalton Laboratory Plan in a secondary school*. New York: Macmillan.
Mayer-Oakes, G. H. (1936, December). Dalton Plan in a small high school. *Education*, 244–48.
Semel, S. F. (1992). *The Dalton School: The transformation of a progressive school*. New York: Peter Lang. A history of The Dalton School still operating in New York City. Foreword by Maxine Greene.

Index

About the Author

JUNE EDWARDS is Professor of Education, SUNY, College at
Oneonta.